HACK THE CORPORATE FAST TRACK

Accelerate your corporate maturity

Erik Newton

ISBN 978-0692518342

Dedication

To people motivated to succeed
and willing to work to make it happen

Table of Contents

FOREWORD

This book is about regular businesspeople doubling their income working in a corporation for a boss. It is not really aimed at entrepreneurs and people who want to start their own companies. Their hack is more of a breakthrough vision paired with unshakable confidence and drive.

Corporate maturity is the most important soft skill and the biggest driver of promotion to the higher levels of a corporation. There are a lot of unwritten rules in business and between people, and some are confusing and contradictory. People seen as mature have understood and internalized these rules. They will be promoted first and fastest.

I have organized this analysis of the major elements and drivers of corporate maturity into four sections. In the first section I lay out the corporate context and a version of reality. In the second, I dive deep into perfecting your relationship with your boss. In the third, we explore how to make yourself more mature sooner. Finally, in the fourth, I provide some general career navigation advice.

This book provides insight, advice, and guidance for individual contributors and managers as they attempt to climb the corporate ladder. If you believe these insights, will you use them to accelerate your corporate maturity and promotion chances?

Erik Newton

I. THE CHALLENGE AND THE OPPORTUNITY

1. Maturity

Maturity is the ability to react and deal with situations and people in an effective way. Popularity follows when you exercise maturity consistently. Corporate maturity is the skill of being effective and popular inside a corporation. And it leads to promotion.

Almost no one would argue against maturity, but many people conflate popular with shallow and self-centered character. Likeable, admirable, respectable, successful people are also popular. There is no contradiction between being popular and being good.

Maturity has a number of primary forms: mental, emotional, relationship, and operational. Mental maturity gives you the patience and insight to figure situations out. Emotional maturity regulates your reactions. Relationship maturity means you mesh with and communicate effectively with others. And operational maturity enables you to get stuff done. Corporate maturity requires all four types, and appreciating that and how much development each requires makes it easier to see why it drives corporate promotion.

To illustrate the impact of maturity, look at immature drivers 16-19 years old: according to CA DMV they are 3.8 times more likely to be involved in a fatal or injury car accident than the rest of the population. What comprises driving maturity? Mental –

good decisions. Emotional – good self-control. Relationship – good interactions and communication with other drivers. Operational – familiarity with roads, situations, conditions, darkness, weather, and car performance. How do people develop driving maturity? Experience, training, temperament, and by paying attention and remembering the close calls and lessons learned from the mistakes of others. Drivers with 29 to 38 years experience have the fewest vehicle accidents. Mature drivers make fewer mistakes and are easier to share the road with. Corporate mature employees make fewer mistakes and are easier to work with.

Look at the effect of maturity in romantic relationships. Immature teenagers will struggle to find a boyfriend or girlfriend and if they do are likely to struggle dealing with unfamiliar issues and problems. A person who has had more relationships will develop the maturity to better handle meeting and dating situations and is more likely to be "promoted" into long-term relationships and marriage. No one wants to drink immature wine or fly with an immature pilot or ride the train of an immature conductor. Immature is synonymous with "not ready."

All forms of maturity require pattern matching, which comes from experience, paying attention, and applying the insights of one situation to another. Corporate maturity mostly comes from family, working, working early in life, good bosses, a bit of luck, and working longer each day than other people. If you start working during college at 18, you will have close to a 4-year head start. If you work 60 **hours a** week after college, you will gain 3 years of experience for every 2 years of average workers. By 28, you will be about 6 years ahead of average performers who start working at 22. Early and long hours is a simple and well-known hack. Let's look at a few dozen more.

2. Angle of Ascent

Before we explore how to accelerate maturity, let's take a look at the environment in which we work. Increasing your corporate salary will require promotion to higher responsibility and titles, and people with the most talent, best work ethic, and most advanced maturity usually get promoted first. Let's say you'd like to double what you make in real terms (net of inflation) in 5 years. Simple compounding math says that you need to increase your capabilities by about 15% every year. Are you 15% more capable than last year? Are you 30% more productive and valuable than 2 years ago? When you look at the input, your talent, before the context, the job opportunity, you get the horse and the cart in the right order.

Increasing your value that fast is a big challenge to deal with, but reality can include additional headwinds to overcome. When a rising tide lifts all boats, your job situation should get better with the same level of effort as last year. But what if human competition increases? Then you have to work harder to stay even. What if, in addition to increased competition, the economic tide is ebbing out because of the drag of increased federal debt, healthcare costs doubling every seven or eight years, hidden inflation, wealth concentration, and cash-strapped state and local economies increasing fees and taxes? What if new technology makes your field obsolete? Making the same next year will mean a decreasing standard of living, which has been the case for about half of US households over the last 30 years, according to the US Bureau of Labor Statistics. Adjust the relative strength or weakness of your field on top of that 15%. If demand for people in your field is 10% below average, you might need a 28% (1.15 / .9) increase in capability to double your income. The math helps illustrates the challenge.

I work at least twice as hard and twice as long as my father did, yet I cannot afford a house in his neighborhood. My return on my extra effort works against the headwind of increased competition, house appreciation (in his neighborhood) outstripping my income appreciation, less effective government, and dramatically higher health care costs. These headwinds require me to do about four times as well as my father to buy in his neighborhood.

Depending on the ebb of the tide, and whether you can maintain continuous employment without a setback, you need to improve your capabilities in excess of 15% every year to double your real income in 5 years. Real income is your salary after inflation. If inflation increases by 5% and your salary increases 9%, your real wages increased only 3.8%. Subtracting the inflation rate from your wage growth gives a rough real income gain number, but the formula is (new wage / inflation rate indexed) or in this case 109%/105% or say $54,500 / 1.05 = $51,904.

Realistically recognizing the steepness of the Angle of Ascent required is the first lesson of the hack. The Angle of Ascent defines how much effort and time you should invest to double up. For a single-income household, failure to move up will likely trap you in the new working class where you won't be able to afford college for your kids without substantial loans or save for a comfortable retirement.

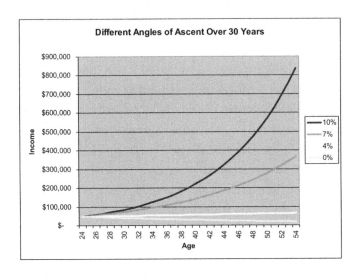

This graph dramatically displays the difference in value acquisition and incomes over time. Starting at $48,000 and increasing value by 10% after inflation takes a person to the C-level compensation of $837,000 by age 54. A person who starts at $48,000 but does not increase their value will see their standard of living fall to under $20,000 in 30 years because of inflation and industry changes, which has probably happened to the millions of manufacturing and mining workers whose jobs were shipped overseas. People who are forced into early retirement will also be in this low-income bind with the added problem of needing more medical care but not being eligible for Medicare until age 62. Nearly 20% of the households in the US make less than

$20,000 a year and 14% of the people, 1 in 7, use food stamps to eat. Medical bills drive more than 54% of US personal bankruptcies, according to healthaffairs.org.

Age and Income Table at Different Angles of Ascent				
Age	10%	7%	4%	0%
24	$ 48,000	$ 48,000	$ 48,000	$ 48,000
25	$ 52,800	$ 51,360	$ 48,480	$ 46,560
26	$ 58,080	$ 54,955	$ 48,965	$ 45,163
27	$ 63,888	$ 58,802	$ 49,454	$ 43,808
28	$ 70,277	$ 62,918	$ 49,949	$ 42,494
29	$ 77,304	$ 67,322	$ 50,448	$ 41,219
30	$ 85,035	$ 72,035	$ 50,953	$ 39,983
31	$ 93,538	$ 77,078	$ 51,462	$ 38,783
32	$ 102,892	$ 82,473	$ 51,977	$ 37,620
33	$ 113,181	$ 88,246	$ 52,497	$ 36,491
34	$ 124,500	$ 94,423	$ 53,022	$ 35,396
35	$ 136,950	$ 101,033	$ 53,552	$ 34,334
36	$ 150,645	$ 108,105	$ 54,088	$ 33,304
37	$ 165,709	$ 115,673	$ 54,628	$ 32,305
38	$ 182,280	$ 123,770	$ 55,175	$ 31,336
39	$ 200,508	$ 132,434	$ 55,727	$ 30,396
40	$ 220,559	$ 141,704	$ 56,284	$ 29,484
41	$ 242,615	$ 151,623	$ 56,847	$ 28,600
42	$ 266,876	$ 162,237	$ 57,415	$ 27,742
43	$ 293,564	$ 173,593	$ 57,989	$ 26,909
44	$ 322,920	$ 185,745	$ 58,569	$ 26,102
45	$ 355,212	$ 198,747	$ 59,155	$ 25,319
46	$ 390,733	$ 212,659	$ 59,746	$ 24,559
47	$ 429,807	$ 227,545	$ 60,344	$ 23,823
48	$ 472,787	$ 243,474	$ 60,947	$ 23,108
49	$ 520,066	$ 260,517	$ 61,557	$ 22,415
50	$ 572,072	$ 278,753	$ 62,172	$ 21,742
51	$ 629,280	$ 298,266	$ 62,794	$ 21,090
52	$ 692,208	$ 319,144	$ 63,422	$ 20,457
53	$ 761,428	$ 341,484	$ 64,056	$ 19,844
54	$ 837,571	$ 365,388	$ 64,697	$ 19,248

Find your income and age on this table. Are you on track for the income you need and want? Are you willing to invest one hour a week to increase your Angle of Ascent? If you are not, go catch some reruns on TV. If you are, read on and put what you learn into practice to increase your Angle of Ascent, starting with understanding the concepts of Deliberate Practice and Feedback Attraction.

3. Deliberate Practice and Feedback Attraction

The 10,000-hours-to-greatness authors, Colvin and Gladwell, make a clear distinction between casual practice and deliberate practice. Leisurely golf or tennis does not advance your game, it passes time and may keep your skills from deteriorating. Doing email, sitting in meetings, and preparing uninsightful reports that few read do not advance your game, but they may keep your income from deteriorating.

Deliberate Practice has three primary requirements:
1. a specific skill goal
2. a target number of repetitions and
3. a clear feedback mechanism

For example, I would like to improve my market research knowledge for use in campaign planning. I will review qualitative, quantitative, and bio-feedback research techniques in three white papers and read our company's last ten research results which used these techniques. I will then prepare a presentation and present it to the director of market research and ask her to score my understanding of the material 1 to 100 with a minimum target of 90. Any areas I am weak on I will list and address within two weeks. That would count as Deliberate Practice and would advance my game.

Feedback Attraction

A friend says, "Nothing gives me as much satisfaction as when people take my free advice." So the obverse must hold true: "Nothing makes me feel like I wasted my breath as when people ignore my free advice." The workplace does not provide people much straightforward feedback. Sure, you can get no response and assume you have mishandled a communication or a project. Giving feedback is tricky because most people do not really want it. Rather than seeing feedback as a tool to move them forward, people feel threatened by feedback and often react defensively. Being Feedback Attractive means you seek it out and show appreciation when it is provided. One of my bosses said, "Feedback is a gift."

Getting feedback in annual reviews often has somewhat limited value. The manager often rushes to provide feedback to many people. Managers force themselves into using the sandwich approach of saying something positive and something negative, and cover problems that may be out of date. Annual review feedback often fails to directly connect to an objective that the person understands well and works towards. Additionally, the review is often connected to the annual pay adjustment, which tends to make the feedback conform to the intended raises.

Attract feedback by simply asking potential mentors: Can I get your advice on something? I am working on improving my judgment / interpretation / forecasting / lateral management skills. What is your take on my current capability? Where should I focus on to improve my capabilities? Can you think of any situations I should have approached it differently? If you ask for feedback, people will understand that their advice will be heard, more likely put into practice, they and will share more valuable insights.

Okay, so 10,000 hours of practice makes you a "genius," but you only need a 10% annual increase in capabilities to make C-level eventually. Working 9 to 5 with a lunch break and taking one hour a day to chat with co-workers, check email and social networks leaves 30 hours of work a week, which is the minimum you probably need to do to not get fired. This allows you about zero hours to work on self-development. Take out vacations, holidays, and sick days and you work about forty-eight 30-hour weeks or 1,440 hours a year. So, your self-development needs to be at least 144 hours on top of that to increase your capabilities by 10%. By the way, 144 hours per year of Deliberate Practice will make you a 10,000-hour genius in 69 years. This kind of math is why Nobel Prizes usually go to people in their 50s and 60s with a median age of 54.

Where will you find the time? Can you expand your work hours by 1 hour per week? If you dedicate 1 hour a weekend to it, you can find about 48 more hours, which should give you enough time to develop and meet a 6.6% 96-hour goal. By the way, if you watch just 2 hours of TV shows, sports, news, and movies per day, you will spend 730 hours a year and you won't be any more awesome than last year. The average American watches at least 4 hours and 48 minutes of TV and streaming TV per day – more than 1,700 hours per year (Neilsen, 2014). Imagine how much TV the unemployed watch. Imagine how quickly they could retrain themselves if they used 1,000 hours effectively. Based on my observations and discussions with others, 144 hours a year is probably more than most can manage, so I am dropping the target to 1 hour per week of planned and monitored practice with feedback. Deliberate Practice with feedback is that much more impactful than studying, observational learning and expertise development.

Let's say I wanted to double my Scrabble score, which I really do because I usually score around 240 and have trouble beating my kids. If I devoted 52 hours a year to doubling my score, how would I allocate the time? I would:

1. Buy some books on Scrabble strategy
2. Memorize all the 2-letter English words
3. Study Latin prefixes and suffixes
4. Expand my vocabulary with word-a-day cards or apps
5. Attend Scrabble tournaments to try to understand top players
6. Watch Scrabble-related documentaries
7. Start doing crossword puzzles, which is important because I would not need a partner
8. Buy Scrabble software that would suggest words and allow me to play against the computer
9. Consider seeking out a Scrabble coach or at least find a mentor with consistently high scores

10. Join or start a Scrabble club to find like-minded people to play
11. Plan to play at least once a week
12. Keep a running list of my final scores to mark my progress
13. Eventually join a tournament and try to survive past the first round

If you ask, most people want to make twice as much money as they do now. So, how much do they invest to double their capability? Most of the people I know go to maybe one or two conferences per year and sit in a training session or two, read a blog or newsletter, read one or two business books, and do one or two projects a year at work that advance their knowledge.

No one I know has an actual business training plan of any kind, let alone one anywhere near as structured and specific as my Scrabble plan above. People count on the passive accumulation of years of experience in known companies to elevate their station and income. The experience accumulation approach has numerous limitations: companies prefer younger workers for most positions because they are less expensive, have more energy and are easier to train. If a person's skills are not developed and they do get a promotion with broader and more complex responsibilities, they are less likely to succeed and risk being fired.

A pianist practices scales and technique. A golfer practices driving, putting, and bunker shots. A football player practices footwork, moves, ball handling, and builds endurance. What exactly do businesspeople practice?

Email? Sitting in meetings? Holding their tongues? Biding their time? Filling out forms? Approving purchase requests and expense reports? In addition to mastering skills in your field, how do you accelerate your corporate maturity to become more promotable?

Reading this book or any other is not practice; it is studying. Practice requires you to have a goal, repetition, and a way to gather feedback. If you don't have all three, don't count it as your 1 hour a week.

So, read on and identify the maturity skills you want to master and make a plan to invest at least an hour a week developing them.

4. Sufficient Plateau and Pre-Empowerment

The Sufficient Plateau is a combination of effort and compensation that people achieve and feel sufficiently good about. It is usually around $150,000 in the Silicon Valley. It happens more often when a person's spouse works and earns the same or more, which essentially doubles that $150k. From the Sufficient Plateau, people attempt the probable: they look for ways to maximize leisure time and achieve a balanced lifestyle. They often look at work as a 9-to-5 proposition. Working 8 hours a day is not a problem in itself, but over-focusing on tactical work with no eye for innovation and Problem Obliteration (explained later) can create a weak spot around that person's function that can lead to others.

Is it each employee's right to work exactly 40 hours and get paid that $150,000? It's a punch-card, factory-worker mentality with the hint of a one-person union. Managing these people is a drag because they are motivated to do just enough to stay on the plateau and stay employed. These people don't mind much if management ignores to stay below the radar.

However, the company's competition may be pushing up and pushing in from all sides, so the company has to take a steeper Angle of Ascent just to hold its ground. If it has a significant number of employees treading water on the plateau, it will lose to companies where people strive harder and attempt to do the impossible every week because eventually they will, and it will allow them to eclipse your company's position and the layoffs will begin.

In a layoff, people who work on the Sufficient Plateau should be right near the cut line depending on management's preference for easy-to-manage or harder-to-manage but more valuable, and the severance packages are distributed. Every sixth or seventh player gets a bust card. In soft markets, Sufficient Plateau people do not find new jobs as readily as steep Angle of Ascent people.

Management should address the Sufficient Plateauers in two ways: One, avoid hiring people who are looking for a Sufficient Plateau. Hire people who show a fire to grow and have high goals. Hire people who want to take your job and are willing and able to try to become capable enough to handle it. In a layoff, don't put the Sufficient-Plateau people above the steep-Angle-of-Ascent people, even though the steep-Angle--of-Ascent people can be more work to manage. Two, management should set the pace by asking people for their whole contribution of creativity, energy, and emotional labor, and dissuade them from measuring performance in a salaried job in terms of hours in the office.

Pre-Empowerment

Did you see the movie *Minority Report?* In it, they use pre-cognition to prevent crime before it happens and live in a nearly crime-free city. In the movie, planning to break the law is the same as breaking it, so the pre-cognition police can arrest and imprison pre-criminals and protect the victims. Recognizing Pre-Empowerment before the crime of doing the mediocre minimum is an early step to being more mature and valuable.

Some people wield the excuse that their lack of a higher title prevents them from doing more. You are Pre-Empowered to be insightful, innovative, curious and all the other traits in this book. Now, that doesn't mean you don't have to be skillful and tactful in how you do it and still build buy-in and align on timing. It doesn't mean you don't have to do most of the boring stuff your job entails and follow most of the established processes in your environment first.

As long as you work for a boss who has not told you ridiculous things like, "assimilate, don't innovate" or shot down multiple well-developed proposals, consider yourself Pre-Empowered to add value. If you work for a de-empowerment boss, look for another boss or another job because you are wasting time.

Working for a no-boss is like playing blackjack and being told you cannot hit on 11 or 10. It's insane. It will definitely prevent you from achieving the Angle of Ascent you need to double your income.

Many make the mistake of believing that the responsibility of management rests solely on the shoulders of their boss and bosses. In a sense this is technically true, but most intelligent people–and you likely fall in this category given your desire to read career-advancement content–understand the importance of managing in many directions, which is the focus of the next section of this book. Before that let's look at a fast track hacker profile from someone I worked closely with.

Hacker Profile One – Jennifer

Education: BA, State University of New York College at Buffalo. She paid her own way through college with limited assistance from her parents by working 30 hours a week and taking on loans and working full time in the summer.

Background: Parents married, stable, middle-class family, youngest of 4 sisters.

Progress: Made director in a public company at 26, senior director at 27, and VP in a different larger public company at 33. She made VP of Communications at her next company before 39.

Jennifer works in PR, so she figured out early how to listen, speak, write, manage big egos, and position her story and herself. Maturity skills were intrinsic to her work.

She selected her career path early in college and had multiple internships in her field of PR during college and stayed on that vertical track the whole time.

Jennifer is an outstanding verbal and written communicator and always quickly returns professional and personal emails and phone calls.

She was a 3-sport team athlete in high school and played 1 sport in college. Works out regularly despite being very busy managing a team of 12 and 2 children.

Motivated, competitive, ambitious, and optimistic.

Jennifer reads 12 books a year and thousands of blogs and articles.

II. MANAGEMENT AND YOUR BOSS

5. Managing Up

Allocate 5-10% of your work time to managing your boss. It sounds like a lot but will generate a return on your efforts. It often takes people years and even decades to realize that management is exercised in both directions. Younger employees usually focus too narrowly on the work from their perspective. As employees start to increase in sophistication, they learn to adjust everything they do to improve communication and execution with their boss and their superiors. Some do this to improve job security and reduce constructive feedback from their boss, but others realize that an excellent definition of their job is: "To make their boss look good." Some younger people might take a cynical view and think they do not want to help their boss look good as they already feel like the boss takes more than a fair share of the credit.

Why manage up and make the boss look good? Assuming the boss is competent, the boss knows what the company and group objectives are and communicates them to the team. When each member of the team hits goals, the team achieves their plan, and when the team does that, it helps the division and company hit their goals.

Consider 4 levels in the progression of managing up: Manageability, Fit, Accommodation, and Anticipation. At the first level, you mostly see the work from your perspective, but you try to do it correctly and enthusiastically. At the second level you begin to see your work from your boss' perspective. At the third level you deliver the work to your boss' perspective. At the fourth level you deliver work that the boss is unaware is needed but recognizes as valuable as soon as you present it.

Going through this process often makes people feel that they are losing their individuality and their ability to make their unique contribution. However, Managing Up allows you to deliver the value your boss and your organization need most, therefore driving success and more appreciation for your work. Consider the following questions carefully and assess your capabilities.

Level 1 - Manageability
1. How easy are you to manage?
2. Do you listen and follow directions?
3. Do you meet your schedules and deadlines?
4. Do you offer to take on lower level tasks to free up your boss' time for higher level ones?
5. Do you do things your boss is not aware of? Do you expect her/his support if you mess it up?
6. Do you know why you are communicating to your boss?
7. Do you provide the proper amount of information back to the boss at the proper frequency?

Level 2 - Fit
8. Do you know your own strengths and weaknesses?
9. Do you know your boss' strengths and weaknesses and do you look for ways to complement your boss' weaknesses with your strengths?

10. Do you do what you are asked and then go farther and deeper?
11. Do you think about what your boss really needs to know at what level of detail to make a decision?
12. Do your explanations make it easier or harder for your boss to make decisions?
13. Do you present solutions as options?

Level 3 - Accommodation
14. Do you look for the intent of what was asked for in addition to what was actually requested?
15. Do you know if your boss prefers email, printed material, or verbal updates?
16. Do you know if your boss prefers numerical or descriptive explanations or prefers documents, spreadsheets, or presentations?

Level 4 - Anticipation
17. Do you consider how your boss will present the material at the next level?
18. Do you consider what your boss might need and prepare it in case you are asked or if the opportunity to present it arises?
19. Do you make suggestions to your boss that help organize and manage complex tasks or processes?
20. Do you identify problems and bring the problem and proposed solutions?

The higher people go in the organization and the more corporate mature they are the more time they spend considering these questions and their answers.

One time I recognized that we were in danger of losing a significant account which I managed. I had a chance to speak to the VP about it and told him my concern. He replied that I should "bring him solutions, not problems." He then walked away and did nothing about the account. We lost the account, didn't get the other bigger account, and many people were laid off. At the time I thought it was the lamest comment I had ever heard. Years later I realized that he was probably right. It would have been more mature if I discussed it with my boss, presented the problem with options, and agree that he would escalate it.

I could have said: As our delivery schedule is slipping, we are in danger of losing this account. Perhaps we should consider one of the following solutions:
   a. Hire more people to get back on schedule
   b. Divert resources working on the more-significant account
   c. Tell the client that we are unable to deliver a product in the category and basically resign the account

Option C was likely the only one that we could have done. In the end we did nothing but slip the schedule repeatedly, and I transferred to another division. 70 people were laid off because of two larger problems and this smaller one.

Release the Mental Holds

Your boss manages a wider sphere of activity than you do, probably 3-5 times more. Since you are fully engaged in your work, imagine doubling or quadrupling the number of things to think about and manage. Managers develop a larger capacity for thinking, sharper memory for next actions, and better speed at executing through completion. The human brain will continue thinking in the background and subconsciously until an item is closed. Open items create mental clutter and lead to stress, fatigue, and mistakes. Take the time to release the mental holds your projects have on your boss's mind as soon as the relevant actions are completed. Forcing your boss to think of the next step, ask you if it has been done, and wait for the reply doubles and triples the mental hold space.

The Collective Brain and Training Your Boss

A well-functioning team relies on each member to develop skills and maintain specific knowledge. The well-functioning group saves energy by not individually accumulating all those skills and retaining all that knowledge. As long as each member transmits information and reacts when needed, the group achieves far greater range and performance by specializing. Your judgment and communication skills are like the neural response in the collective brain. Slow and ineffective responses will create an effect like a stroke or senility on the collective brain; it will function but with diminished capacity. Swapping that low-function individual for a better one will improve the collective brain's "health" and performance.

You expect your bosses to be more talented, experienced, and knowledgeable than you and to train you and help develop your career, right? However their greater breadth of responsibility requires them to decrease depth in each of the specific areas they manage. Do you look for ways to train your boss on your area and feed a steady stream of useful, current, specific knowledge from your area? Helping your bosses understand insightful details of your work will increase their ability to appreciate your achievements and explain their value throughout the organization. It helps no one if your boss provides partial explanations that create misunderstandings, confusion, and unanswerable follow-up questions.

Recently one of my reports found a research paper that she thought I should read. She printed it out, highlighted it, and gave it to me at her one-on-one. I reviewed it and found it valuable and took it to my boss, who reacted very positively and asked for a digital copy. The following day, we included references to the tactics covered in that paper in a presentation we prepared for the CEO. Her willingness to train me quickly reached the CEO three levels above her and transmitted part of that collective knowledge. When was the last time you presented a highlighted article or paper to your boss?

Talented bosses value upward knowledge from their reports and will likely invest more training time and energy in their reports who train them.

Coachability and Trusting Your Boss

Do you trust your boss? If not, and you do not because your boss is untrustworthy, then look for a new boss. If you never trust your bosses, then look to yourself to develop trust skills. One way to exhibit trust is to be coachable. Take direction and suggestions from your bosses literally and do what they say. Doing nothing or doing something other than what your boss asked for indicates a lack of motivation, listening, or trust.

> I had a report who rolled out a presentation to other departments without showing it to me first. It was incoherent and damaged the credibility of her, me, and our group. After the presentation, I asked her to always show me material before it left the group and get an active approval. She reacted very negatively and said that meant she didn't "own" any of her work and that I only wanted to make sure I looked good and that I didn't trust her. I said that I totally disagreed with all of her conclusions and that over time she would understand why. The next month she showed me the presentation and practiced presenting. I told her it was confusing and hard to follow and helped her restructure it. After she presented to the group that second month, I heard from two of the ten people that it was an outstanding presentation and that you could prove it because the VP did not ask any follow-up questions or issue any new action items. The following month we made further refinements. She practiced her delivery three more times on her own.

Her presentation was so good that the VP emailed me while she was doing it to tell me it was "a great presentation." That VP very rarely uses the word great in that way. Later, I forwarded the email to my report who beamed with pride and satisfaction. Her reputation with the VP and SVP improved substantially, which benefited her personal interaction with them, her job satisfaction, and her compensation.

So, she does not "own" her work, the *company* does. That's why it pays her to come in. I wanted to make sure *she* looked good, so I looked good and other groups respected the quality of work our group does. And it was *she* who did not trust me completely. The dramatic difference in the reception to her work and praise from the VP made it clear to her why we review material before distributing it, and why it makes sense to trust what a good boss says and to do as requested, even if you don't at the time understand why.

You expect your boss to coach you, but how coachable are you? Do you listen well, take notes, follow directions, and practice? People may not mind teaching you something once, but they will become impatient and irritated if they have to repeat it a second time. After that, they will stop coaching you because they feel like talking to you wastes their breath, or they begin to see you as a lost cause. Companies should consider getting rid of the uncoachable because they have a far lower future value than coachable employees. Poor listening and uncoachability are signs of corporate immaturity.

Getting Promoted

Getting promoted is harder than you think. Way harder. Half-level promotions–like manager to senior manager–without material changes in responsibility are sometimes given for tenure and retention. Aside from battlefield backfill promotions, senior manager to director or director to VP promotions require you to outperform a significant number of other people.

If you have ever asked your boss, "how can I get promoted?" then you may have experienced one of the most uncomfortable and awkward meetings of your career. Your boss probably started answering the question contextually with something like: "it depends on the situation and the person;" clearly an accurate answer but of absolutely no use whatsoever. If you persist with a clarification such as, "well, how about for me in this situation?" then the answer you heard probably made you feel like you were falling through the looking glass. The glaring contradiction is that most of the time the company wants you to do the job you want to be promoted to before you are promoted. But, unless you are in the top 2.5%, you are not getting any training for the position. At the same time, your boss restricts you from doing overscope work because it is not your job or responsibility and you would bump into people if you did, most notably your own boss. Remember, your boss is also trying to get promoted, so s/he would prefer as few variables or wild cards in play as possible. No one will ever say it, but bosses are also reluctant to promote people because it, to a very small degree, increases the competition for their promotion.

There is a possible contradiction in your motivation. While you want to seem as promotable as possible, you do not want to seem like you focus too much on getting promoted or that you are too much for yourself.

The company also does not want to promote people because it increases the payroll and the stock comp costs and makes the company more top-heavy. More top-level people can also make decision-making more cumbersome and time consuming.

> I asked the "how-to-get-promoted" question on behalf of one of my reports to my SVP, which didn't at the time strike me as perilous. He scheduled an ad hoc meeting with me. He came into the conference room with a sour look on his face and a large envelope. These were two things I was not at all happy to see. He smacked the envelope down and glared at me and said, "So he wants to be promoted, huh?" I clarified that he wanted to know what he needed to do get promoted. He glared at me some more. He thought about it and said, "there is no set criteria for it, and I have never heard anyone answer that question, but let me try to answer now." As he started to talk, I relaxed and stopped thinking that he was going to fire me for asking. He outlined the criteria in the list

below, which included a number of very non-obvious points.

You need to:
1. Be operationally proficient at everything in your current job
2. Be at least ~50% proficient at the job you are to be promoted to
3. Show an indication of the additional value the company will get from promoting you
4. Develop strong working relationships with a wide array of people
5. Be a person other people naturally follow and would want to report to
6. Have broad-based support from your peers; they want you to have more authority
7. Produce results that are tangible and valuable to the company
8. Exhibit sound judgment and make few errors
9. Display a positive and constructive attitude
10. Exhibit excellent communication up, down, and laterally
11. Be effective, especially at getting other people to work on your projects
12. Innovate actively and reinvent your job as needed
13. Contribute more than is asked of you and more than your peers
14. Outperform everyone else at your level
15. And beyond that, the company needs to require your promoted services, so timing and a little bit of luck matters also.

Note that about half of his promotion criteria relate to corporate maturity and relationships. By the time he was finished, I was a bit surprised at how difficult it seemed, and we were satisfied that it was still somehow fair and aspirational. Oh, and the big envelope? It was a retention bonus for me. Cash is far easier to get than a promotion.

Promotion can be a mystery and there rarely is a map to guide you. Earning promotion, somewhat counter-intuitively, also requires a person to effectively Manage Laterally.

6. Managing Laterally

Getting colleagues to complete their part of the work on time is a great source of frustration each person faces. Managing Laterally requires all the skills of Managing Up and more because you lack the same close working relationship and direct inter-responsibility.

A person who can manage laterally will soon become widely regarded as someone of high impact. Effective lateral management requires use of a broad range of tactics and the ability to modulate constantly from one tactic to another until the work is completed.

The Source of Delay

There are probably 100 reasons for delays, but here are some top culprits. Understand how you use these delay tactics and try to eliminate them from your work environment; you will see huge speed gains. Delays are so common that anecdotes about delays are unnecessary in this section. After each source of delay in the list below, I have added a countermeasure. Most of the countermeasures are the responsibility of management or team leaders to foster and implement.

1) **Delay in starting**. Also known as procrastination, delay in starting is the foundation of delay. > Take action as soon as the plan and responsibilities are clear.

2) **Lack of a plan and specific schedules.** Planes and trains would rarely arrive on time without knowing the expected arrival time. > Put "Plan"

and "Schedule" on the agenda whenever one is needed.

3) **Lack of prioritization.** Some people lack the ability to address the big rocks first and go for the little ones to look busy. > Ask "Which are the top priorities?" before starting project work.

4) **Unidentified delivery date.** This will make the project nearly impossible to prioritize and schedule. > Ask "When is it due?"

5) **Too many producers.** This dilutes work, satisfaction, ownership, and accountability. People like to disguise their laziness in groups and big meetings. > Try to keep teams small, identify the roles, and designate a lead for each project.

6) **Too many approvers.** Ask enough approvers and the directions will start to go in circles. > Ask your boss or the highest-ranking person who gets the last word. Inform all the approvers who else is approving and what their comments were.

7) **Delay in approval.** It often takes longer to get approval than it does to do the work. > Relentlessly pursue approvals. Calendar appointments for review and approval.

8) **Complexity.** It often makes projects feel harder than they need to and creates multiple points of failure. > De-scope to scale the speed and productivity.

9) **Confusion.** People give up really easily if they do not understand what they are doing or why they are doing it. > Confirm directions and repeat often – 4 to 7 times.

10) **Lack of prior investigation.** Though delay in starting is a prime cause of delay, some projects require an appropriate amount of investigation to scope correctly. > Plan to do the investigation separately and before locking down the plan and schedule.

11) **Overscope.** Large projects have a compounded chance of bogging down and imploding. > Right-size the projects for speed.

12) **Scope creep.** You can never succeed if someone keeps changing the definition of done. > Use a backlog to divert creepy requests.

13) **Low transparency.** People sometimes purposely hide project information and details to prevent other people from having input or taking control. > Force team to put data in common areas. Train team to circulate news, good and bad. Over-communicate.

14) **Friendliness and selfishness.** People who try too hard to get along imperil projects by keeping quiet instead of speaking up about risks and potential mitigation. > Reward people who put the project and the company's goals first.

15) **Tinkering for perfection.** People often invest resources without evidence that the change they seek will impact performance. > Test hypotheses, distribute data, and disabuse people of their narcissistic delusions of subjective superiority.

16) **Lack of trust.** Distrust enables people to develop and operate hidden agendas. > Have an open

culture. Team build. Encourage professional-personal relationships.

17) **Fear.** Personal security trumps group success for some. > Encourage risk taking. Reward the risk takers.

Managing Laterally

The primary lateral management skill is holding people accountable for their commitments. The primary tactical areas fall into five categories:

1. Preparation
2. Context
3. Confirmation
4. Follow Up
5. Escalation

Preparation: Doing thorough preparation sets the stage for making a clear request; it builds your credibility and sets a higher standard for other people's work. Preparation includes: collecting and reviewing all related documents, especially those from prior attempts or executions and reading them to make yourself at least as knowledgeable on the topic as anyone else in the company. You should also meet with people involved in prior attempts and collect their input, especially on what didn't work or stopped the project last time. Find all the data and numeric analysis you can. Initiate some preliminary conversations and identify the correct people to involve, schedule a meeting with a clear agenda, and send out preparation questions and background documents.

Context: Communicate to colleagues what you want to do, why you want to do it, and how it fits in with larger objectives. Mention how it has been done in the past and whether or not it was successful. Identify the roles and make sure people agree with their roles in the project.

Confirmation: At each step in the process repeat action items for confirmation in person and send out meeting notes with action items, owners, and most importantly deadlines. When actions and deadlines are agreed to, take these critical steps: 1) ask the person if they are confident that they can hit the deadline, 2) get them to agree that if they don't hit the deadline that they will contact you directly and provide a new target date. Taking these two steps will dramatically increase the lateral accountability.

Follow Up: Follow up is the true core of managing laterally. At each stage, agree on the next steps, and let the other person know that you will contact them just before the deliverable is due. If a deadline is missed, switch gears and ask them to specify the new delivery deadline as agreed to in the Confirmation stage. Follow up relentlessly every day and modulate modes of contact between email, phone, stop-by meetings, and scheduled meetings.

Escalation: Escalation is an effective but expensive tactic. You can escalate up your chain of command or up their chain. You can escalate in email or in person or in a conference call. When you escalate, you can increase your control and minimize collateral damage by asking your boss to intervene on a specific topic with a specific goal with a specific person unless your boss has input on whom to address it to.

These techniques help you get lateral work executed:
1. Being well prepared, thoughtful
2. Documenting thoroughly
3. Making priorities clear
4. Making member roles clear
5. Descoping or resizing when needed
6. Modulating mode of communication: email, phone, drop by, scheduled meeting
7. Asking for target date as someone commits
8. Asserting target date to complete
9. Secure passive approval: "Unless you object in writing, we will move ahead with this version."
10. Copying others to create peer and org pressure
11. Not copying others, email only one person
12. Calling out individual names for specific responses or action in a group message
13. Being clear on budget
14. Offering funding for needed resources
15. Setting expectations
16. Securing and applying executive sponsorship
17. Sharing bigger context, strategy, and fit of project
18. Building your own credibility by always hitting your own deliverables and deadlines
19. Showing appreciation, praising others, sharing credit
20. Developing stronger personal relationships
21. Escalating to your boss or their boss or both

The **RASCI** model is an established team-management technique that breaks down the team roles and responsibilities in a clear and helpful way as follows:

- **R**esponsible: the owner of the problem/project
- **A**ccountable: the person to whom "R" is Accountable and the authority who approves to sign off on work before it is effective
- **S**upportive: provides resources or plays a supporting role in implementation
- **C**onsulted: provides information and/or expertise necessary to complete the project
- **I**nformed: needs to be notified of results but not necessarily consulted

Winning People Over

Securing approval and support from other people is one of the most important capabilities and requires corporate maturity and people skills. When we sell ourselves and our ideas and secure support, it means that other people are buying into us.

Early in my career, I was not good at this. Looking back, I may have alienated more colleagues than I won over. I lost patience with people who could not see what I saw or disagreed with me or were lazy. My solutions were to go over people's heads and to do their jobs for them. The first tactic makes people resent you; the second one people dislike, but doing their job in your spare time is difficult for them to make a big stink about. If you do other people's work, some of the craftier colleagues will intentionally start to delay in order to get you to do more of it.

At one job we needed some data processing done, and there was a charming receptionist in the office on a short-term contract. We asked her if she wanted to move to the data project once she was done. She said she did, and I assigned a senior report to manage her. He very patiently trained her and she started to run the project. I noticed that she got along better with him than anyone else did. In fact, she seemed to make him docile and made it easier for all of us to get along with him. This intrigued me, so I started to watch them communicate to see what her secret might be.

My marketing group sits together at eight facing desks with no cube walls, so we can all see each other's faces while we work. The group is made up of vertical experts, two of whom are engineer-types, who nearly frown in concentration while they work. They are more likely to smile at a heady joke or a good zinger than when they approach another person for a favor.

The first thing you notice about Erin is that she smiles a lot when she talks. She speaks fairly quietly and always uses a pleasant tone. You can't always hear what she is saying, but you can kind of feel how she is saying it and see the person she is speaking to smiling and being won over.

One day I asked Erin directly about her communication skills and asked her if they were innate or learned skills. It is easy for someone like me who does kind of poorly at something to chalk up the gap to natural gifts or a different upbringing.

Erin said that they were definitely learned skills. She said that when she was younger, her parents warned her about her tone and choice of words, but like most teenagers she did not listen. Through college she got jobs in restaurants as a hostess, cocktail waitress, and server, so she had many chances to win upset customers over–hundreds of hours in fact. You can see where this story fits in with the book.

I asked her to explain all of her tactics to me and her answer went way beyond what I was expecting:

1. Smile
2. Use a pleasant tone
3. Compliment other people
4. Choose your words before you enter a conversation with someone. She said she might spend ninety seconds planning her words before engaging her manager in a three-minute conversation
5. Don't complain
6. Don't gossip and bad mouth people
7. People like eye contact, so she opens her eyes wider when she wants to win someone over.

I asked her if she did all this consciously and she said, "Yes, but it also has become a habit." I asked her if she used this on me and she said, "Yes." I asked her if it works on everyone or just men. She said, "It works on both men and women."

She told me a story of a time a drunk woman got aggressive with her at a concert bathroom and started to pick a fight. Erin thought quickly and said: "Oh, I love your purse and your blouse, where did you get them?" She touched her arm and then her hair and said, "Your hair looks great." The woman settled down and the problem was averted. Maturity and communication skills can solve all kinds of problems.

Erin is a black belt at winning people over, and she has mastered a skill that every corporate fast tracker needs. Her advice applies to management in every direction, even when Managing Down.

7. Managing Down

The basic elements of managing down are staff meeting, 1-on-1, quarterly planning, personal planning, annual performance review, salary adjustment, and, in Silicon Valley, bonus or stock grants. Personal development is the responsibility of the employee, and management should invest development efforts in those who show high potential for promotion. As a manager focus on a clear plan, employee engagement, and removing blockers and demotivators.

In his book *Drive*, Daniel Pink explains that attempts at external motivation have limited impact and external motivation usually dampens internal motivation. That means that money, stock, praise, fear, and feedback have limited net effects on performance and can even deter it.

The desire to be promoted, gain responsibility, and earn more is the significant driver to contribute above the mean. Yet 3 in 4 employed people have little or no promotion aspirations. An October 2012 survey by OfficeTeam found that 76% of workers do not want their boss's job.

I suspect the number of people who want their boss's job is higher for single breadwinners and lower for people who have sufficient assets or those whose spouse has significant income.

Statistics and normal distribution tells us that 84% of people are in the bottom 4 standard deviations, so they are neither inclined nor qualified to manage and lead. These people calibrate their exertion for optimal instead of maximal performance.

Statistically normal distribution of data is consistent with the promotion survey above.

So, only 1 in 4 college-educated, qualified people are even interested in or motivated by promotion. It follows that 3 out of 4 qualified people you hire should not be and do not want to be promoted.

A typical division has a 1 C-level, 1 SVP, 2 VPs, 8 directors, 16 senior managers, 24 managers, and 24 coordinators, contractors, or vendor consultants. In this example, 11 or 14% of the people are executives and 64 or 86% are not. About 16% of the 86% or 10 of the non-executives are high performers who will move up. 72% of the total people will probably not become managers, but the company needs these people to maintain operations.

That means that 3 of 4 people should not be managed to high performance. It's largely a waste of time. The time should mostly be invested in the 25% who are high performers. Low performers regard management as micromanagement; high performers regard it as coaching. It's a no-win situation to closely manage middle and bottom performers.

The highest performers are in the top 2.5%. These people end up in that bracket in a variety of areas from education (summa cum laude) to sports (champion competitors) to hobbies (run marathons, triathlons). The top 2.5% earned over $350k in household income in the US in 2013. In a company of 1000 people about 2.5% (A+s) or 25 of the people are fast-tracking and being given special development attention by management. The next 12% (As, A-s, B+s) are given consideration for promotion, but little development attention. The rest are necessary but interchangeable workers. It is said that As hire As and Bs hire Cs. Don't promote Bs. They'll bring the organization down.

The key is to hire a larger-than-normal share of high performers. To increase the chances of recruiting and retaining high contributors, look for and interview for these traits.

1. Self-education and a thirst to understand
2. Adaptability, flexibility, positivity
3. Competitiveness
4. Desire for promotion and salary increase
5. Highly productive and scalable
6. Impact, influence, and relationship skills
7. Cultural fit

Self-education and a thirst to understand
In interviews, I ask people what business books they have read in the last twelve months and find most candidates read between zero and two. That tells me they are not self-educating. Candidates should be able to cite newsletters and blogs they read and reference some recent learnings. I like to find that a candidate has researched a topic by gathering white papers, contacting industry contacts, and drafting presentations or delivering talks within their company.

Adaptability and flexibility and positivity
Fast-moving industries change, so I like to find that people can scale up to managing multiple projects without getting overwhelmed.

I ask candidates to name three colleagues and ask them to provide three adjectives they would use to describe the candidate.

Competitiveness
I look for evidence of self-motivation in their hobbies for goal setting and achieving. I like to hear that people train for sporting events, set reading goals, climb mountains, and study for advanced degrees and certifications.

I ask candidates, "Who was the highest performer in your last organization and how do you compare yourself?"

Desire for promotion and salary increase
Desire for more money usually translates into a desire to be promoted, so I like to hear that a candidate has a goal and desire to earn more.

I ask that tired, old question: "How much do you want to earn in three and six years from now?" And add, "How do you plan to achieve that?"

Highly productive

A very productive employee contributes three times more than an average one. I look for people that play fast, decide fast, look for and fill holes, and share data. I ask if they write their goals, how many they have, how many they achieve, and how many more they could have achieved and under what circumstances? What have they done in their current position that surprised their boss or colleagues?

Impact, influence, and relationship skills

I like employing people who make things happen. I ask candidates:

What cross-functional project have they led?
What new projects have they proposed?
Who do they struggle with in their current role?
Who are their allies and why?

Cultural Fit

The term "cultural fit" is the new catchphrase for likeability, drive, and corporate maturity. The old term was "team player," which always sounded like sell out and get along to me. I never found the term team player used by high-performance teams and organizations, just the mediocre ones. I like the less judgmental "indoor skills," to indicate a set of skills people on teams in corporations develop and get used to that people who work by themselves usually do not. Catchphrases aside, I look for collegiality, collaboration skills, coachability, and listening skills.

In an interview in addition to situational questions about experience and skills I ask:

How many of your colleagues do you interact with for work? In situations besides projects?

What was the last feedback someone gave you? When was it?

What did you do with it?

Unfortunately, interviews are statistically the least accurate method of predicting future performance. Interviewers have such deep biases and interviewees have prepared answers, so true insight is limited. Most managers have no better than a coin flip track record of hiring high performers. One of my reports said he hired 8 of 10 high performers and proves his success by showing that 6 of the 10 made vice president in their subsequent companies already. One of them is covered in a hacker profile in this book.

Once you hire good people, provide them direction, context, and feedback; and don't neglect to build trust and delegate. Have a weekly staff meeting. You set the meeting, you set the agenda, and you lead. Have a weekly 1-on-1. Your report sets the meeting, the agenda, and they lead.

Context

Management happens in a context that comes from the corporate culture, the HR department, the top executives, the division executives, and the manager.

Feedback

Develop criteria and provide them feedback on their progress quarterly. Annual reviews are too infrequent to make an impact.Build Trust

There are many ways to build trust. Most of them boil down to acting with integrity and keeping your word.

Delegate

Give people projects and direction and let them find their own way to the finish line. If they fail, coach them and give them easier projects next time.

Management

Managers are responsible for hiring, evaluating, compensating, and guiding employees. Employee performance comes from the individual.

Use a ninety-day evaluation period to weed out weak people from among new hires before they get embedded. Fire or lay off the lowest 5% of the company every year. That will keep people on their toes and raise the average performance of the company. It will prove that there is a consequence for under-performance. Encourage tenure for most positions to be six years or less. Keep people in roles for two years or less.

You can only manage people to do a little bit more than they will do organically and in the time it takes you to get them to do something, you could probably do it yourself. The more you manage, the more likely you will be accused of micro-management.

Spend your time managing context, culture, setting standards, and inspiring people by setting a good example in your work ethic and practices. Hire self-motivated, competitive people. Focus on leadership instead of management. Get people to manage for results instead of for activity.

Micromanager or Microemployee?

The bogeyman of workers everywhere, micro-management is the go-to term to describe detail-oriented bosses who get too involved in their team's work. Every time I ask my team what they look for in a boss or what they expect, "not micromanaging" comes up first. What is micromanagement? If you ask the people who say they hate it, they will have some trouble defining it, like: "monitoring my work, nagging me for schedule updates, editing my work, changing things that don't seem important, forcing practice presentations, and giving detailed advice on how to present, or forcing multiple rounds of revisions." Most of what they come up with sounds pretty much like management to me.

Micromanagement is an over-involvement in the process of getting work done or the over-focusing on subjective changes to the work that are unlikely to make a difference in quality or results. Micro-management reduces ownership and accountability. The problem is not micromanaging itself, but the implication of it, which is that the work is not good enough, that the person is not competent, and that the boss does not trust the team member to figure out how to make it better.

The part team members fail to recognize is that they may actually lack the experience and talent to produce excellent work and that they may not in fact be competent at a task or overall. Neither competency issue is easy to accept. It is much easier to blame the boss for being a meddler. Micromanagement is most often used as a remedy for marginal people who do marginal work. When someone is performing below satisfactory professional standard, management develops a plan to improve their skills and performance. Since the person is challenged, it takes a lot of work at a detailed level to try to improve the performance. The people who complain the most about micromanagement are probably the weaker employees, and they are likely the employees with worse attitudes, the ones who are likely to make more negative comments about all of the work conditions. Micromanagement takes more of the manager's time than it does the staff because the manager has to consider what to say and deliver it and evaluate it.

The part bosses fail to recognize is that not trusting your team makes them aim low and stunts their growth. They will continue to disappoint you if you do not develop them to the level where they will produce great work. Further, you have to recognize that not trusting them squashes their motivation, wipes out their value-add, and makes them prosthetic hands for the directions you give them.

If the team members are not competent and do not seem re-trainable, fire them. If you as a team member are certain that your skills and work are outstanding and your boss makes the work worse with micro-management, quit. One of you is wrong, and more often than not, you will find it is the team member.

Despite what I just wrote, I can relate the following:

I was in a company and reported to the VP of Marketing. He got fired and then I reported to the CEO. He and I worked rather well together and I made the best of it, but after working with him for a few months, rather than figuring out myself how to make things excellent, I asked him for his input and did what he wanted. It was easier and faster as he was very likely to greatly alter any work he reviewed. The behavior was well known throughout the company, and rather than arguing things out, directors and VPs usually ended discussions and disagreements with, "Let's see what the CEO wants."

After six months, they hired a new VP of Marketing and he preferred me to do my own work and was comfortable letting me make my own mistakes. People around the company started to notice that I seemed happier and more energized. I said I liked my new boss and we got on great. After a few months, I needed to finalize a video script and scheduled a meeting with my VP, my CEO, and me. My VP was late, so he told me to go ahead without him. The CEO and I started to go over the script draft, which he didn't read, and he then mapped it on the whiteboard and made me his prosthetic hands to write it. He used a tone that was dismissive. His version was mostly the same. He dampened my motivation and sense of ownership. The meeting was a bore, and my interest and accountability for the project dimmed. Though I liked him quite a bit, that tone and management style would be why I would leave the company a few months later.

This may have been one of the rare cases where the team member was competent, but the boss was a hopeless micromanager—this was the first script I had ever worked on. The video, for the record, turned out awesome thanks to all three of us.

So, if you are a team member and you do not want to get micromanaged, become a mature, popular, macroemployee. Consider trying the following: ask for very clear directions when a project is assigned, ask for sample work to model after, plan for iterative review cycles on specific dates along the way, ask questions for clarity separately from delivering the work, deliver the work ahead of the planned milestones, have other people check the work before the boss, ask for feedback on the delivered work, and schedule time to review and enhance the work with your manager. Start project conversations with, "I'd like your advice," or, "I need some additional direction," or, "Do you have any suggestions for..." Preparing to avoid a lot of detailed management requires a lot of work, doesn't it? Are you not that thorough while at the same time accusing your boss of micromanaging? Perhaps the problem is that you are a microemployee or are microlazy. Do you describe yourself as a big picture person and a big thinker? Guess what? Almost no one has that job title. The CEOs I worked with usually read all of their email and responded in minutes. U.S. CEOs read an average of sixty books and articles on best practices a year. You too, right?

Additionally, try to keep control of the editable version of what you are working on by showing it on screen with a projector. When reviewing, if your manager starts to redo the work, politely say that you now understand better what is required and that you would like to take next edit and review it together at the next milestone. If you do all that and the manager still redoes your work and makes you dispirited, ask yourself if you know what you are doing and if your work truly is good. If the answer is yes, then find a new boss.

If you are a manager and you want to avoid micromanaging, give work to people who have appropriate capacity, give clear instructions, provide examples, set milestone dates, give general feedback on the work including negative feedback—and offer to collaborate. Always make sure the team member does the editing, express confidence in the person, and show appreciation for the progress made even if the work is not yet satisfactory or excellent. Most importantly: ask questions—all kinds of questions—so that the person gains insight and learns and expands and does not find you a lecturing, tiresome bore. If that does not work, change the person's function or fire them. You have better things to do than tactical staff work.

Polite Dissatisfaction and Constructive Impatience

Have you had that boss who seems impossible to please and lets you know it each time you deliver work? Did you ever stop to think why? Most would say the boss is not a good manager. Or sometimes your boss is far more talented than you and not at all shy about reminding you. Part of an executive's job is to set and drive the standard of quality and performance. Even if the work is well-developed, an executive might send you back with it to make sure it is the best output the organization can generate.

Rude dissatisfaction is demoralizing. Polite Dissatisfaction sets the standard above what was just delivered. Take the dissatisfaction as feedback. See it as a challenge to exceed your current capacity and ability. Express Polite Dissatisfaction, especially with younger colleagues or reports to elevate their performance. Give feedback like, "This is a good start, but I suspect you could do even better work if you took another pass at it." Raising standards is like steepening the Angle of Ascent: if you don't do it, you will chase a competitor who has.

Have you heard of the triple constraint? Fast, Cheap, or Good. Pick any two. Managers have to optimize between the three and fast is often the aspect that can be addressed without totally sacrificing the other two because work is often unnecessarily slow. Constructive Impatience helps turn up the heat and the tempo on the project owner and participants. With the heat turned up, people are more likely to air out current roadblocks and red tape that a manager or an exec can clear. Project durations should realistically reflect the actual amount of time required to do the work. Some people should focus on speed and throughput while others focus on quality and details.

Wouldn't it be annoying if the dealer only dealt four hands of blackjack per hour? You'd say something, wouldn't you? So, let colleagues who are missing deadlines know that unnecessary delays do not work.

Most team performance failures are the fault of management; one, for not setting a high enough standard, two, for not communicating it clearly and regularly, and three, for not holding the staff accountable by removing people who do not perform when one and two were not adequately done.

Business failure starts with low expectations. People want to get the most pay for the least effort. They look around and most of them will aim for the median level of performance but due to self-overestimation will deliver less value than they intended. If most people come in at 8:55, so will they. If most people under-prepare for presentations, so will they. If most people work until 5:05, so will they. If most people do not advance the standards of what they do, they won't either.

Setting and enforcing standards and setting strategy are the primary jobs of the executives. However, managers at all levels have to actively communicate and enforce their expectations to staff, vendors, and partners. When expectations are not met, managers must stop and address specific points of failure. Although it is uncomfortable to communicate expectations at the point of initial failure, broader failure is worse.

Examples:
The deadline is in two days, what can we do to ensure that we make it?
We agreed to create the report and discuss it at this meeting, didn't we?
My boss expects…
I am disappointed at…
I am frustrated that…
I feel like we are not on the same page…
I think we can do better…
Good start, but I'd like to increase our focus on…
Can we agree that next time we will…?

Prolific business writer Seth Godin describes the origin of great work in two words: "Don't settle." The act of settling shutters the great work in while propelling the mediocre work on. Balance quality and speed and modify that to, "Don't settle too soon." Godin also asserts that the best people deliver high-quality, vested, emotional labor.

Professional Urgency

Urgency is an insistent feeling and mode focused on completion of a task with both immediacy and speed. The feeling compresses execution time (by elevating the clarity and intensity of communication), overcomes obstacles and objections, and identifies solutions and next steps. Organizations and groups of people require more urgency to make progress because increasing the number of people slows a project down, dilutes accountability, and increases complexity. Urgency helps identify the fastest route to an acceptable solution instead of relying on the safest or most familiar route to a supposedly perfect or appropriate solution.

Dilution
Groups move slowly because people become less certain of who should do what tasks. People in groups are more cautious because mistakes are visible to and affect more people. Organizations usually reward caution and penalize courage and risk taking. The reward for taking risks is usually limited with a slow earn-in period. The penalty for taking risks is nearly unlimited and can have an immediate rejection or ostracism response; promotions take years– terminations can take only hours or even minutes. In groups, credit is distributed and people worry about blame if there is a problem.

Complexity
A single person thinks and does, revises, completes and measures project time in hours. With two people, sometimes one thinks, the other does, they have to

match schedules, discuss, revise, compromise and decide together when it is done. They have to be careful to listen and understand and try not to offend each other. That could easily take four times longer. When you add a third person, it could take twelve or sixteen times longer. Add a fourth and you have a committee and the time required goes from days to weeks. Add another group or committee and the time to completion may go to months. Add another group in another organization with a different culture, like a non-profit or a government office, and it may take quarters to complete. Throughout this increasing complexity, ownership and the satisfaction that comes with making something is lost. The complexity of adding people can have an exponential lengthening effect on completion time.

Resistance to Change
Projects often cause change. People who value the status quo often resist because they prefer the current situation. These people need to be removed from a progressive organization.

Laziness
Some people resist work because they are lazy and apathetic.

Dilution, complexity, resistance to change, and laziness are the major anchors on project progress. Professionally urgent people make clear requests, overcome bogus objections, identify effective next steps, create schedule deadlines, and hold themselves and others accountable. The larger the organization the more valuable professional urgency becomes.

> I had the opportunity to practice urgency when I handled a request for a new web page. The next day additional requests came in that made the web page more complex and increased the expected development time. The engineers requested the content assets by the end of the day. I went to the content producer, and she said that she would be able to provide the content three days later. I knew that would make the development difficult and increase delay. The content producer suggested using placeholder text and images, but my sense of urgency made me ask if it would be okay if I took a crack at drafting for her review and approval. She said okay, so I started asking her questions about the benefits and features. I had to restate my question four times to get enough material to start writing. I had a draft for my boss to review two hours later and the content was delivered to Engineering on the schedule they requested.

Urgency affected the interactions, reactions, ideation, activity, owners, roles, sequencing, and output of this project. Without professional urgency, I might have gone back to the engineers to see what they could do if I delivered the assets three days later.

The next section of this book switches focus from managing others to strategies to managing yourself. When it comes to hacking the corporate fast track, it is conceivable that the only thing more important than being effective at people management is self-management through accelerating your corporate maturity and capability.

Hacker Profile Two: Mark

Education: BA in Business, Michigan State University. Put himself through college with little assistance from his parents while working full time. Graduated with honors in 3 years.

Background: Stable lower-middle-class family with 1 younger brother and 1 older sister. Parents factory and service workers. Parents married for 37 years.

Progress: Made director in a private company at 23, senior director at 26 and VP of Marketing in a different, large private company at 30. He then became a private equity marketing executive at large before 35.

Worked full time from the age of 16. Worked in some aspect of marketing whole career.

Mark works tirelessly late after hours and early before other people get to work.

Mark is an outstanding written communicator and always returns professional and personal emails and phone calls.

Mark is motivated, competitive, and ambitious.

Keys to his success: Hard working, positive, likable, and insatiable desire for knowledge.

Mark is country-boy humble.

Mark reports that he reads 4-5 books a year and thousands of blog posts.

III. ACCELERATE YOUR CORPORATE MATURITY AND CAPABILITY

8. Goalset Optimization

Simplistic, immature thought and behavior pursues a single goal to the exclusion of others. Food, water, sex, and money have a long history of finding singular fulfillment sometimes at great expense to other goals, like health, reputation, relationships, and staying out of prison.

Sophisticated thinkers and workers learn to simultaneously optimize multiple goals rather than pursue only a single one. In business our primary goals revolve around sales, profit, growth, output, quality, speed, innovation, service, brand, reputation, relationships, personal likability, and security.

Pursuing one goal is easy: maximize that goal. If you run a sprint, you want to maximize your speed. In an ultra-marathon you probably want to maximize your distance. Between two goals it is reasonably easy to make trade-offs as the impact from one goal to another is rather visible and easy to comprehend.

The triple constraint is well known in development, construction, and most service industries, expressed by the triangular resolution: "Fast, Cheap, or Good–pick any two." This construct resolves the constraint by eliminating one of the goals, which is effective but simplistic. What if you have five goals and multiple stakeholders require all five to be considered and addressed?

In business, we usually need a goalset optimized, for example:
1. Sales
2. Profit
3. Speed
4. Quality
5. Relationships

You cannot maximize five vague business goals simultaneously, but if you add specific targets it gets easier. For example:
1. Project Sales – $2 million
2. Project Profit – $400,000
3. Speed – Released by June 1
4. Quality – Defect-free product
5. Relationships – Existing customers and employees happy

Now, you can better see that all five of the goals conflict with at least one other goal. Sales won't go up without a Quality product and marketing spend, both of which make Profit go down. Speed cannot be achieved unless employees agree to work overtime. If you push the schedule too hard then Quality can suffer.

Optimizing requires compromises, so most people will ask to list the goals in priority order or to assign weights. Once that is done you do some simple scenario analysis:

Approach A, Approach B, Approach C

Most intelligent people can then make a good guess as to which approach best satisfies the goalset. Mathematically, you can go farther and score the expected efficacy of the five goals and targets one to ten within each approach and multiply them by an assigned weight between zero and one and create a weighted score for that approach. The highest scoring approach maximizes the goalset.

Recently my boss explained that to be a VP, you have to focus on the goals of the company over your department's goals–to think like an owner. This is difficult when the company puts pressure on you to achieve your department goals to be considered a success and be promoted. The maneuver requires you to shift fluidly and reweight the most important goals dynamically. Let's call that Dynamic Goalset Optimization.

Average employees pursue one outcome at a time; valuable mature employees can pursue many. Make yourself a more valuable, sophisticated, and subtle employee and consider the team's or company's goalset instead of your one goal. To do so, ask, what about 'this' goal? enough times to identify the right goalset and targets. Establish priorities and weights and then build a plan to optimize for all the goals simultaneously.

Prioritization is the ultimate clarifying tool in business. Use it to decide what to work on, in what order, and, also very importantly, what not to work on.

To prioritize focus daily on these elements:
1) What are the stated priorities?
2) What priorities did you commit to?
3) Where do you connect to other groups to deliver on priorities?
4) Where could you help others achieve theirs while still staying aligned to yours?

Use the clarity of your priorities to politely decline to engage in projects that are at odds or distract from achieving them.

And once you understand your goalset, and priorities, Start with Yes.

9. Start with Yes

"Yes" is what any person making a request of you wants to hear. Say yes to every legitimate business request your boss makes of you. This in no way means you should lie, it means *provide the best solution possible given the constraints*. This is probably the most valuable advice in this book. If you remember only one thing, remember this: people like, respect, and promote people who say yes and provide solutions. People who start with yes are more popular. Solutions are what the company pays you for. Almost no one likes the person who sees all the problems, tries to mitigate all the risk, and is able to forecast all the project failures. Even if well intentioned, those people associate themselves with the problem instead of the solution. Everyone knows it is easier to say no and stop an initiative than come up with a new one.

A few jobs ago, my new boss asked me if we could be ready to take customer service calls for the partner campaign in thirty days. There were a lot of reasons to say no:
1. Not enough time for training
2. Not enough agents to take the calls
3. The staffing plan is made ninety days in advance
4. Not enough time to stock the new product
5. The project was unlikely to generate significant sales volume
6. Based on the forecast the hold time would be much longer than target

There were also reasons to say yes:

1. The call center is up and running and agents are familiar with the pitch
2. The call forecast was based on an overly optimistic projection
3. The partner was price-sensitive and the projected costs were high
4. My boss asked us to do it and told the partner we could do it

My staff started preparing to say no. I told them to say yes. Specifically, we said, "Yes, we could take calls in thirty days but hold times might get long if call volume was high initially." This was perfectly true within the constraints and showed us playing offense instead of defense; defense frustrates bosses and executives. Our answer satisfied him. The next day the partner said that for the cost we quoted, he would prefer to do it internally and the project largely ended. That is what my boss expected. The big loser would have been the person who made the boss reverse his commitment on the date for a project that would actually never begin. The boss would remember who sent him on that errand.

This section may seem at odds with the prior section on Goalset and priorities, so add a step where you consider the priorities and point out when a request from your manager is inconsistent. If they still want you to do it, agree to adjust the priorities first, Start with Yes, and then get on with the task.

Almost always say yes and provide the best possible solution given your constraints. In doing so, you will establish yourself as reliable, positive, and solution-oriented, which will add to your credibility and trustworthiness.

10. Aim for 10 Times More

The next section also focuses on optimization through an exploration of a well-known productivity analysis by Steve McConnell. By recognizing differences between the best and worst employees, programmers in this example, we can extrapolate 10 approaches for you to follow to see a ten-fold increase in your own productivity.

Exploring "Individual Productivity Variation in Software Development" by Steve McConnell

"In the late 1960s, Sackman, Erikson, and Grant conducted the original study that found huge variations in individual programming productivity. They studied professional programmers with an average of seven years' experience and found that the ratio of initial coding time between the best and worst programmers was about 20 to 1; the ratio of debugging times over 25 to 1; of program size 5 to 1; and of program execution speed about 10 to 1. They found no relationship between a programmer's amount of experience and code quality or productivity.

This degree of variation isn't unique to software. A study by Norm Augustine found that in a variety of professions–writing, football, invention, police work, and other occupations–the top 20 percent of the people produced about 50 percent of the output, whether the output is touchdowns, patents, solved cases, or software (Augustine 1979). When you think about it, this just makes sense. We've all known people who were exceptional students, exceptional athletes, exceptional artists, exceptional parents; these differences are just part of the human experience. Why would we expect software development to be any different?

Team Productivity Variation in Software Development

Software experts have long observed that team productivity varies about as much as individual productivity does--by an order of magnitude (Mills 1983). Part of the reason is that good programmers tend to cluster in some organizations, and bad programmers tend to cluster in other organizations, an observation that has been confirmed by a study of 166 professional programmers from 18 organizations (Demarco and Lister 1999).

In one study of seven identical projects, the efforts expended varied by a factor of 3.4 to 1 and program sizes by a factor of 3 to 1 (Boehm, Gray, and Seewaldt 1984). In spite of the productivity range, the programmers in this study were not a diverse group.

They were all professional programmers with several years of experience who were enrolled in a computer-science graduate program. It's reasonable to assume that a study of a less homogeneous group would turn up even greater differences.

After reviewing more than twenty years of data in constructing the Cocomo II estimation model, Barry Boehm and other researchers concluded that developing a program with a team in the 15th percentile of programmers ranked by ability typically requires about 3.5 times as many staff-months as developing a program with a team in the 90th percentile (Boehm et al 2000)."

This quote is interesting and explains why some people get ejected from the work force despite having years or decades of experience: *"They found no relationship between a programmer's amount of experience and code quality or productivity."*

Simple experience alone is not enough. It is better to think, plan, and develop yourself in terms of skill, maturity, and productivity. Experience matters for operational maturity when combined with the pattern matching capabilities that allow a worker to be more productive with the work and more effective with teammates.

There is a lot of data above, which lays the foundation for Aim for 10 Times More. Here is my prescription for 10 Times More productivity outside of software development: double your performance in ten areas and you will easily make a ten-fold increase in your productivity.

1. **Double your goal management time.** You will be more than twice as clear on your priorities and what you need to do.
2. **Double your focus.** Develop the discipline to stay on task and do not get distracted. Improve your concentration. Make lists of to-dos and check them off. You will get more than twice as much done.
3. **Double your preparation.** Most people spend just a few minutes getting ready for the day or for the next meeting. If you double your preparation, you will notice twice as many connections and be able to contribute twice as much in a meeting.
4. **Double your curiosity.** Think of and ask more good questions. You will know more than twice as many important facts.
5. **Double the feedback you collect.** You will understand yourself better than people who collect it once a year and will be able to make a number of times more adjustments.
6. **Hold yourself and your teammates twice as accountable** and cut your use of excuses in half. Stop working around people and broken processes.
7. **Double the courage you allow yourself and take more chances.** You will get more than twice as many good opportunities.

8. **Double your determination.** Fail twice as much and twice as fast. Succeed four times as often.
9. **Double the quality and positivity of the people you spend time with.** Support the success of teammates and the team.
10. **Double the appreciation you express to the people who help you.** Their help will remain steady or increase.

If each recommendation only doubles your original capacity, the ten together will make you ten times more effective. However, these skills will multiply with each other and provide you even more gains over time. It is an explanation and a formula for why some people contribute 10 times as much and make 100 times more than the bottom 10% or 20%.

Another reason people get stuck in the bottom percentiles–and it may seem entirely obvious to you as someone interested enough in improvement to read this far in a book on the very subject–is their failure to become experts and to evolve their knowledge.

11. Be an Expert and Evolve Your Knowledge

By developing expertise you make yourself more valuable. Pick an area that includes specialized information and for which you see demand and above-average wages. For example, differentiating cooking expertise is difficult because much of the population cooks and believes they can do it to a competent degree. However, far fewer people write computer code, yet proving that expertise is difficult in conversation. Intellectually authoritative people do an excellent job of helping people think about new and difficult topics or think strategically. They do this by first understanding some non-obvious information through research, experiment, and experience. Then they explain it in simple and straightforward ways that usually include a simple graph or graphic and easily-understood examples. Experts provide useful frameworks that fit right into their listeners' heads and make them feel more knowledgeable and competent. In other words, easily recognizable experts are good at teaching. Are you good at teaching?

I met Dan Greenberg, founder and CEO of Sharethrough, a leading practitioner of viral video distribution. Dan went to the whiteboard and drew a horizontal line to explain the viral potency of a video. The points on the line described how motivated people were to share a video they had seen. This made a lot of sense and helped sort out types we had seen at one end or the other -- pretty valuable already but just a line. Then he drew a vertical line, so he had an X and a Y axis. The vertical line described the degree of brand visibility in the video. This construction describes a universe of hundreds of millions of videos and becomes an indispensable sorting tool that is nearly impossible to forget. Can it be that easy to impress people? Yes, it can. Understand, simplify, add originality to the points on the lines, and then walk people through the expert neighborhood you have created. People respect and like people who help them become smarter.

Updating your skills is a matter of survival. No matter what industry you work in, it changes and evolves. New laws are passed, like Sarbannes-Oxley, that impact lawyers, accountants, and finance people. New technologies emerge, like web sites, search engines, social media, blogs, and user-generated videos that affect newspapers, magazines, TV studios, and everyone in marketing and many in sales. New tools and resources emerge that help productivity, like word processing, spreadsheets, presentation software, email, and mobile devices with apps, which can affect everyone. It is probably difficult for you to imagine not using any of those tools, yet none of them existed thirty years ago. However, if you do not have a computer in your home, which many of the low income 20% do not, you probably cannot use most of these new tools and resources. If they are required for employment, you will not increase your income and quite likely struggle to be employed at all.

Work presents a contradiction. Unique and specialized vertical skills are in demand with fewer competing jobseekers, which provides easier employment and attractive salaries. However, demand for those skills and specialties will wane as new ones emerge.

> Examples of too many years of specialization are easy to see around you. For the first 6 years of my career I used my Japanese skills to work at Dentsu, a large ad agency in Tokyo, and at Adobe Systems in San Jose, managing Japanese accounts. I saw other people in my field getting stuck in doing the Japan work and getting passed over for promotion. I decided to make a jump to domestic work. Lateral jumps usually pay the same or less, but they are necessary to Evolve Your Knowledge.

You can see people in every field facing this danger. In engineering, mainframe design and programming did not translate easily to Linux and cloud computing. Knowledge of Fortran and BASIC did not help get people jobs in Java, Flash, and AJAX. In marketing, if you only buy media in a single channel, you will be in trouble if that channel is overtaken by an emerging one. To get a job in search or email marketing, you need to develop expertise and specialization, but if you do only that for more than five years, you will probably have trouble getting a management job that oversees three or seven channels. It will be less painful to take pay hits when you are making less money. Watch out to keep yourself from getting handcuffed by higher wages that don't provide a viable way upward and keep lateral move timing in mind as you manage your career.

Evolve Your Knowledge by studying adjacent fields to your own and proposing projects in the evolving areas. If you cannot get approval from your boss to do a project, start a small side business and practice the new skills. Alternatively, study and develop a white paper to give to other people interested in the same topic. This will provide you a way to mention that you have done research and accumulated knowledge in that field. Add the white paper to your resume and discuss it at your next job interview after which you can give notice to that boss who did not support your evolution.

Evolving your knowledge helps you layer on the next hack, building credibility and trust.

12. Building Credibility and Trust

Consciously or subconsciously, people always judge each other. Basically, you either meet, exceed, or fail each time you interact professionally with other people. Building Credibility does take time as people require you to accumulate a certain number of entries in that unconscious ledger they keep in their head for everyone other than themselves. Even if you really impress someone once or twice, many cautious and credible people will still want more interactions to make sure they have made the right read on your capability, your reliability, and your intentions.

Professional people – the ones who maintain regular employment – will usually meet expectations by doing roughly what was expected roughly on time. That is the key to maintaining their jobs. People running on the fast track exceed expectations by over-preparing information and analysis, exceeding the level of rigor in the environment, and sweating details like statistics, organization, and information presentation.

Your credibility drops each time:
- Your presentation equipment fails and you do not have a backup
- You forget to bring something to a meeting
- You exhibit an inappropriate emotion, like anger or frustration
- You provide information that later turns out to be inaccurate
- You fail to answer reasonable and related questions

Your credibility plummets each time you:
- Make excuses
- Get caught lying or hiding information

Recently we found that the marketing automation platform had not been updating the CRM and a few hundred customer records were stuck. My director investigated and identified that the change had been caused by a very junior manager. I asked the manager to look at it and fix it. He fairly quickly pointed out that "it was not his fault" and he had never touched the setting. The director confirmed again and sent me screen shots of the change under the manager's login. In a private meeting I brought it up to the manager and he said "it was not me" but he would reset it. I said the screen shot showed it happened from his login. He said a third time that "it was not him." Then he said he had never been trained on that function so it could not be him. I started to count how many times he did not accept responsibility for the fairly minor issue and each time he denied it, I told him the count in real time. Incredibly, he denied responsibility and argued 8 times in that meeting. I finally said, "Can you imagine how frustrating it must be for your manager to hear you deny responsibility 8 times?" He paused and said yes. Later in writing he said he found the root of the problem and added again that he had not been trained on it.

Not accepting responsibility for a situation where someone has taken a sober look at a situation and is working on resolving it is incredibly immature. The damage to your reputation and relationship from arguing outweighs the minor gain from shifting part of the blame. Mature people accept responsibility and focus on repair and prevention not vindication. Even if you accept more blame than is completely accurate, handling the situation well and smoothly should net you gains in credibility, trust, and maturity that have more value. Making excuses is usually more damaging than blame-shifting is helpful.

Credibility gives your actions more force and power. Once you establish credibility, trust soon follows. Study and learn from life every day. Watch for hidden actions and unspoken words. Study body language, especially the signs of disagreement or deception. Choose your words carefully, especially your commitments. Indicate clearly when you have reliable data and when you are making a best guess.

Recognize that it is easier to fail than succeed. Successes span time as they grow, evolve, and attract people to share the credit. Failures close in on themselves, necessitate disposition and attract no one to share the blame. Failure is easier to understand and easier to attribute. People are stingy attributing success to others but generous apportioning blame. So plan and prepare to make your successful interactions at least seven times more frequent than your unsuccessful ones or the negative ones will hold you back like a bag of bricks.

In addition to displaying expertise and enabling others to understand and think strategically as described above, the other key to Building Credibility is to exceed expectations. That upside surprise jolts people into holding you in higher esteem.

In my new employee onboarding class, I met Ryan, Hacker Profile Four. He was a 21-year-old recent college graduate from a strong private university. Near the end of the training week, Ryan created a study guide for the exam and distributed it to all the other students. I was happy to have the guide and glad to be included. I updated the guide with some additional points from my notes. Once we started working, Ryan established himself as the top outside caller in the company. He usually made his weekly target by Wednesday or Thursday. Before he turned 22 he was asked to start co-leading a regional sales group. On the weekends, Ryan wrote articles for the company blog. Ryan introduced dozens of people to recruiting as employee referrals. Later he offered to help me update the database of companies and logos of our customers. Recently Ryan decided he would hit double quota one week because he was out of the office the following week. He set a record for the fastest promotion to account executive in company history. His name has become synonymous with "high performer" and "model employee."

87

Needless to say, his credibility is extremely high, and his opinions carry a lot of weight for a first-year employee. Not only does Ryan possess a high degree of credibility but he also possesses Intellectual Toughness, a quality that ultimately contributes further to his credibility as it has led him to understand a fairly complex software at a granular level.

13. Intellectual Toughness

Intellectual Toughness defines a level of mental discipline that is both intense and focused on finding an answer that raises the standard of understanding and enhances your ability to interpret events and predict outcomes. The Intellectually Tough will dig for information and analyze and reanalyze it. They might find and purchase a research report that might answer the question or contact industry colleagues to see if they have insights or actual data. The Intellectually Tough will propose and run a scientific test to prove a hypothesis. They will partner with people with other skill sets and develop advanced statistical analysis to understand causality, allowing them to forecast and predict future events.

The Intellectually Tough will attempt feats they do not yet know how to do. They accelerate their knowledge gain rate and push themselves to breakthroughs. They do original work that will mesmerize their boss, or if not, their next job interviewer. The breakthrough may only take a few hours of additional work, but once they walk through that intellectual door into the house of greater knowledge they become a bigger player in their field. The next time the subject comes up in a meeting, they can share an insight so far ahead of the current argument that people quickly retreat or defer with comments like: "That sounds interesting, I'd like to see the data." After the meeting they can distribute the data. However, probably far less than half of the people from the discussion will study it thoroughly and understand it. Many will read the abstract and take it as true. The rest will wait and see if no one else shoots it down, and then it will become the new base understanding and shared position. People will refer back to it to resolve future disagreements. This generates significant and valuable credibility for the Intellectually Tough.

Another word for toughness is tenacity, which is even more rare these days for a number of reasons: laziness, complacency, entitlement, and a general fear of being aggressive prevail as many people hold a belief that getting along with people best protects their job security. Unfortunately, they are correct that they will be able to protect their job only if they work for an inattentive boss in a less-than-excellent company, which makes protecting that particular job less valuable.

Have you heard that U.S. high school students rank 40th in the world in math and science? However, they rank first when asked the question: "Are you good at math and science?" Carol Dweck's research on the growth mindset found that children should be praised for effort and not talent; perhaps the aforementioned survey results are due to Americans mistaking the finding as meaning "children should be praised despite a lack of effort and talent."

Intellectual tenacity leads people to look for and understand hard data and root causes. The intellectually tenacious will pursue information that others regard as unattainable or not useful. We study theory in school because the real world will present us problems that we have not encountered before and that theory will provide us a backstop to push off of and go at the problem. The tenacious will use every means, will absorb failures, and will keep attacking the problem until it gives up some insights.

> One of my bosses at a start-up described me as a dog with a bone and she advised me to let go of the bone sometimes. I did. We all did. The company was shut down a few months later.

Intellectual tenacity and hard data, when presented without excess complication to colleagues and chronic skeptics, immediately raise the credibility of the Intellectually Tough and help solve important problems.

Hard data will subsume whimsy and hope, so deliver it gently without adding too much of your own editorial positioning.

5 Steps to Become a Better Thinker

In the business world, your intelligence may be your most important asset. You can enhance both your intelligence and others' perception of your intelligence and wit with these 5 tactics.

1. Ask questions
2. Become a skeptic
3. Don't fall for simple explanations and categorization
4. Become a serious reader
5. Be a real-time, full-time student of life by studying people and situations

Questions and curiosity form your critical thinking. As you listen, think "why?" As you think, think "why not?" As you evaluate, consider the facts and their sources.

When those questions expose gaps, politely ask questions out loud and let people know that you are not in agreement until those questions are satisfactorily resolved. Skepticism is seen as the opposite of gullibility.

Simple explanations and categorization are convenient ways to organize and remember events and circumstances, but careful understanding of complications and subtleties requires mental dexterity and will resolve problems.

Be Curious, Ask Questions

The habitually curious always want to know more about a subject or a person. How does it work? Why does it cause this or that reaction? Curiosity drove every scientific discovery in history. Someone asked a new question. Someone set up experiments and interpreted the results. And someone got the "Eureka!" lightning bolt and in that instant they became the first and only person in the world to gain that new knowledge.

Most people are not habitually curious. They have had their curiosity dried out of them by schools, parents, and peers who found it easier to restrict them to the mainstream path of conventional thought. Sufficient Plateauers avoid asking questions because it usually leads them off their path of minimal work and least resistance on which they prefer to travel. Habitually curious people ask more questions, read more non-fiction works, and trade in the currency of ideas instead of trivialities. Instead of "why should I?" their brains ask "what if?" and "why not?"

Regularly ask yourself questions during the workday. If they seem like good questions, ask other people too. Ask open-ended questions: How should we approach it? What do you think are the keys to success? Ask closed-ended questions: What was the lift last time we tried it? What was the base case?

Making curiosity habitual will lead you to more insights and breakthroughs. The knowledge, breakthroughs, and credibility will increase your value.

The habitually curious are like steel. They ask questions that educate themselves, their peers listening to the answer, and perhaps even the person being asked the question as well. Steel sharpens steel; being curious, surrounding yourself with the curious, and supporting the bold are means by which you can fortify yourself, your team, and your company.

Hacker Profile Three: Mike

Education: BA University of California at Davis, MBA University of San Francisco.

Background: Upper-middle class family with 1 older brother and 1 younger brother.

Works in sales and has for 10 years. Made VP at 40 and now manages close to 100 people as he runs one of the top sales demand systems in technology.

Smiles most of the time. He laughs frequently even while dealing with issues and problems.

Mike is an outstanding verbal communicator and always returns professional and personal emails and phone calls promptly.

Mike is shorter than average, so he is adept at focusing and projecting his voice. His voice makes an impact that helps him achieve his objectives and gives him the ability to scare people when he needs to.

Outstanding, tireless listener. Consultative.

Mike is motivated, competitive, and ambitious. Not at all political. Driven yet also very balanced.

Keys to his success: Hard working, positive, likable, gritty, and relentless.

Mike reports that he read 5 books a year before having kids.

14. Fortification

Think about the people you like best. How do they make you feel? Do they make you feel: liked, appreciated, smart, talented, interesting, helpful, useful, capable, stable, secure, validated, and happy? Some combination of these rolled up as feeling confident? And when you feel these positive emotions–this confidence–you feel stronger and more powerful. How does it impact the amount and quality of work you do? How do you treat the people who make you feel this way? You probably go out of your way to let them know that they are likable and talented and wonderful too, right?

This fortification forms the basis for all your most high-functioning relationships. Let me illustrate:

> Dave is my cycling partner. We both started riding a few months apart. He returns all calls and emails, is always ready to schedule a ride, arrives on time, smiles and shares positive stories, and seems to enjoy my company. I always feel like his top priority on ride days. We switch off planning rides and riding first in a head wind. We push each other to go a little farther and we recently rode one hundred miles on a single ride. Sometimes when my determination or strength wanes, I just look at him cranking away and figure I can keep up and keep going. Dave and I figuratively and

physically fortify each other and achieve more together than we could apart.

Contrast Dave to a friend I'll call James. James calls infrequently, returns emails and calls sporadically, is hard to tie down for a date to go out, sometimes cancels, and seems to have a number of priorities higher than me. This friend jabs and criticizes me because our characters and styles are very different, maybe opposite. His delivery of feedback leads me to defend myself and make counter-complaints. We enjoy each other's company when we finally get together, but we do not fortify each other.

At work, we have a number of key structural relationships, the primary being our boss and our direct reports. The number one reason people quit their jobs is because they don't like their boss. And how do bad bosses make people feel? Unappreciated, weak, threatened and stressed–in a word, unfortified.

Now take ownership of this issue. How do you get your boss to fortify you? Stop and think about this. The answer may be too obvious.

How much time do you spend fortifying your boss? Do you show concern for your boss's challenges? Do you do extra work that helps your boss look good in front their boss? Do you give positive feedback and encouragement when they do something well? Do you crank harder when they have lost momentum to pick up the slack for them? Or, do you, like almost all employees, just lament the fact that they do not fortify you?

Ah, the shoe is switching to the other foot. Are you a Dave-employee or a James-employee? Be honest with yourself. And if you are a James, and nearly everyone is, then why would you expect your boss to be a Dave? You are either charging people's batteries or you are draining them. If you drain them, they will avoid you. If you charge them, they will seek out more of your time and invest more in you. Divest yourself of the self-defeating practice of not liking your bosses and like them instead. People who like people are more popular, right? Don't you like the people who like you better? Fortification explains why. Fortify your key people with words, actions, information, and deliverables. Make yourself part of their inner circle and part of their brain trust. Build a fortress between you.

Aside from fortifying your relationships, you can, though it may seem less obvious, also increase your luck.

15. Double Your Luck

Do some people succeed because they are luckier than you? That is a popular excuse for not trying harder. If luck makes a large difference, then effort matters less. Can you increase your luck? Research shows that lucky people have a number of traits in common:

1. Action
2. Relationship
3. Intuition
4. Attitude

Lucky people do a wide range of reading, collect info for doing more activities and try, try, try. Their motto is, "You can't win if you don't play." One woman who reports winning three contests per week explains that she enters about eighty during that span.

Lucky people are people-oriented. They establish and maintain relationships and invest their time in other people. Each club you join and participate in increases the number of people familiar to you by dozens. Each of those people knows about 300 other people, so your network grows by 3600 one-hop people connections per dozen new acquaintances. Think about how much luck can come from that network.

Lucky people seem to make fewer mistakes, right? But how? Lucky people are good at paying attention to their intuition. They pay attention to their feelings about people and the way their gut feels or if their hair stands up. My wife has good intuition about people and business. I have learned to follow hers if I do not have a strong intuitive read on a situation. Strengthen your intuition by being observant and reflective.

We always hear about positive attitude or visualizing our desired outcome in popular works, like *The Secret* or *The Power of Positive Thinking* or *The Law of Attraction.* Once we gain clarity on what we seek, we are more likely to see it if it passes in front of our faces. One researcher found that being relaxed and open makes us less likely to miss the good luck right in front of us.

> Decades ago in Tokyo I was crossing a busy crosswalk on the way to work. I saw something shiny on the sidewalk. It was either a square battery or an ingot of gold. Defying social customs of not looking like a beggar during the commute in front of your own office, I bent down and picked it up. I could immediately tell by the density that it was an ingot of gold and put it in my pocket. I took it to the police station and after sixty days waiting for someone to claim it they released it to me. I sold it to a jeweler for $130.

Do you want to be luckier? Read, scan, be active, build and invest in relationships, strengthen and use your intuition and maintain a positive and open attitude. By engaging in more activities you will also have more opportunities to learn, and it likely goes without saying that for most people it is easier to remember things by doing as opposed to learning through any other means.

16. Remember by Doing

Most people have an 85/15 rule for information they encounter. They forget or ignore 85% of it within a few days even though they at one point found it valuable. Cognitively, the brain does this to save energy and streamline storage and recall efforts. The brain represents 2% of the body's weight and consumes nearly 20% of the body's oxygen and 25% of its sugar energy.

Your brain is a selfish, lazy resource hog. Have you stopped to listen to how many reasons it can come up with to not go to the gym? *It's too cold. It's too hot. I ate already. I already showered. My leg hurts. I think I am getting a cold. The gym is too crowded. It'll be hard to park. My music player isn't charged. I need to be home for a delivery.* In addition to lazy, your brain is also a coward and it hates exposure to the possibility of failure or embarrassment, so "No" to making new friends, "No" to public speaking, and "No" to becoming awesome. The brain would rather have an easy hit of dopamine from food, chocolate, sex, alcohol. or a tranquilizing couple of hours of television. Your brain overstates your virtue and understates your vice. It is trying to keep you from killing yourself with guilt and remorse because you are its host.

Forcing new information and habits into the easily accessible part of your brain requires application and repetition. People call this muscle memory. Since the muscle cells have no cognitive function, I say muscle memory is the successful subjugation of the lazy brain to use easily re-accessible storage for new information and habits. How many times did your parents tell you the things you now do habitually and regard as valuable? Two? Doubt it. Five? At least. Nine? Now you're getting there. Eighteen? Probably.

> Why is it easy to remember songs and so hard to remember a list of French verbs? In seventh grade I learned a German song in music class. I remember every word of it right now, but I don't otherwise speak a word of German. I took French for three years and can barely use it. The difference was that by adding a melody and five hours of repetition, the German song was granted a permanent visa from my brain and all that French only got a tourist visa and was forced to return home a year later.

I want all of my favorite knowledge accessible like that German song. How do you apply the knowledge from this book or any other idea you embrace? Write it, speak it, share it, teach it, do it, and repeat. It's not a memory technique; it's a battle of wills against the lazy brain. Use knowledge, talk about it, take it on outings, bring it to parties, let it guide and define who you say you are and aspire to be. Live it five or six times and it will become experiential remembering.

> When I was a kid, we didn't have seatbelt laws or child seats, so we would roll around in the back of the station wagon or hang out the windows, like the dog. For some insane kid reason I decided I wanted

to touch the weeds on the side of the road as we drove by. Moving at fairly slow speed I successfully touched one once. Only once. That weed whipped my finger so hard that when I snapped my hand back in tortured pain, I was glad to see the fingertips still there. I never did that again. That's experiential learning.

So you can stick your hand out the window of the car of life and get some quick and painful lessons or assign fifty-two hours of practice per year to learn and practice what makes people mature and popular and remember by doing. Your choice. The former will leave you complaining about how much your hand hurts, and how often do you hear people say in earnest, "I love how much that person complains!" By making yourself a yes-saying, doing, remembering lucky machine, you will feel more positive in general, and exuding positivity will in turn make you more memorable.

17. Memorably Positive

Most people gain satisfaction from being negative and complaining. It is their way of proving to their brain that they really know the difference between good stuff and bad stuff and the act of complaining relieves them of the responsibility of making more good stuff.

While nearly everyone likes to complain, almost no one likes to hear other people complain. Think about a meeting that became a gripe session or a day traveling where your travel companion fell apart and made an off day awful.

People are tired, working hard, dealing with family, and trying to avoid spouse fights. When tired people encounter negativity, it drains their energy further. Consciously or subconsciously people will dislike and start to avoid negative people. Notice the average level of positivity around you and then exceed it, so you stand out to other people as a memorably positive person.

Project positivity. It's pretty simple; you may remember it from kindergarten: Smile, make eye contact, greet people, use positive adjectives when people ask you how you are, provide encouragement, and praise good work. Act available to people when you are busy. Say please and most importantly, say thank you, a lot.

18. Robust Joy

When do you perform at your best in your work and interacting with people? Is it what you do, what you think, or what you feel that brings out the best you?

Read the following and note your reactions:
> *I love what I do, and it doesn't seem like work to me. I like the people I work with.*
> vs.
> *I am so busy and have a lot of pressure.*

In the first case, work flows easily from you to other people and back. In the second case, work requires constant effort, and with everyone feeling the same it will take longer to complete any task. Emotions drive the first case; behavior and tasks drive the second case. What if you put your emotions first and even make them the objective of your efforts? Which emotion would work best for a goal?

I have some questions about the congruity of the goal of being happy and achievement at work. To me this sometimes seems like a technique for scaling back efforts and goals in the face of obstacles or a way to reframe unsatisfactory results. I usually have trouble seeing how happiness gives my efforts specific momentum. I like passion, and other people say that they do too, but I have found that it introduces blind spots and an intensity that can make people uncomfortable. Love is a popular and positive emotion but is too awkward an emotion to focus on and discuss at work. Enthusiasm works well and usually has the right effect on me and on other people. What is it that people like about enthusiasm? It exudes positive energy that charges others and pulls them along without being too heavy or oppressive. Enthusiastic people are usually clear-hearted and rarely carry a hidden or political agenda, so they seem trustworthy and help other people feel at ease. Is enthusiasm a feeling or a mode? It seems like a way of behaving and therefore does not quite serve my purposes as a targeted outcome.

Big emotions can be difficult to describe. Try explaining joy before you read the next paragraph. Don't peek.

It's kind of like love, but is easier to manifest without focusing on another person. It's like happiness but much bigger and deeper. It is like enthusiasm but more sustainable. It's like passion but without the excess heat.

Joy is what I feel when I communicate with people I like who also like me. Joy is what I feel when I am creative and innovative or when I am completely satisfied with my achievement. Joy makes my work seem effortless. Joy is big and generous. Joy is what I felt each time I identified an idea for a chapter in this book and then captured its essence in prose.

Robust Joy is my term for the state that comes from caring both about the people you work with and the quality and quantity of work you do. It is that caring that amplifies and accelerates your capability to do excellent work. You don't work for money; you work for people and for the joy of work and creation itself.

Sublime joy is my term for the state of contentment so mesmerizingly deep that you feel perfectly satisfied without any activity. Sublime joy is more august than robust joy and slightly mysterious, but robust joy will help you get work done and advance your worldly causes.

Allow yourself to care about people and especially your team; develop a robust sense of joy in working together and you will produce better work, faster, and it will give you more satisfaction.

Hacker Profile Four - Ryan

Education: BS University of Southern California. Was student body vice president. Ryan put himself through college with minimal assistance from his parents, some assistance from his grandmother, and by working full time and taking on substantial loans.

Background: Parents still married, stable upper-middle class military family, father was a lieutenant colonel, mother is a doctor at a non-profit clinic, has 1 younger brother and 1 younger sister.

Progress: Ryan is in the fourth year of his career after entering at the age of 21. He has been promoted six times: from enterprise business representative to account executive to competitive overlay to senior account executive to top account executive to director of strategic accounts.

Ryan almost always smiles and his eyes exude energy and enthusiasm. Ryan works tirelessly late after hours and early before other people get to work.

Ryan is an outstanding verbal communicator in every way and always quickly returns professional and personal emails and phone calls.

Ryan is Asian-American humble, but his top-dog confidence occasionally outshines his humility. For his +1 at President's Club he took his grandmother to Hawaii.

Keys to his success: Hard working, positive, likable, gritty, driven, and has insatiable curiosity.

10 More Outstanding Traits

1. Idea Attentiveness

You are a knowledge worker. Cherish and nurture ideas and good questions.

> Once I started idea-storming this book, I went to take a shower and I had a great idea for a section. Then I had another idea and forgot the first. Once I realized I forgot the first and started trying to recall it, I forgot the second. Ideas can get away, but not if you write them down.

Being idea-attentive means you keep a small pad of paper with you and write your ideas and To Dos down before you forget them. Everyone knows this technique but almost no one does it. You can also email the ideas to yourself from your computer or mobile device. Practice by writing one idea you generated from reading this book. Really write one down. Write it on anything. Right on this page if you want. Don't read the next section until you do.

2. Attention Surplus Disorder and Professional Seriousness

Estimates place the proportion of people in the U.S. with attention deficit disorder at 4.7%. Whether you have ADD or not, you can have ASD, Attention Surplus Disorder. It is characterized by excellent listening skills, the ability to confirm directions, and re-edit until a job is done to a professional standard. ASD sufferers take the time to clarify and prioritize and are prone to being slightly ahead of the requested schedule. A fairly rare condition, ASD is highly sought after by corporate, non-profit, and academic administrators.

Staying in business is serious business. The majority of all companies started do not survive more than thirteen years. Staying in business is a life and death struggle against fierce odds. Since you are not the CEO or the owner, do you feel like, "if it doesn't work out, I'll get another job?" The top boss doesn't feel that way because the company is an entity and s/he feels the seriousness of the responsibility to keep it alive and enable it to provide for the dozens or hundreds of families it supports.

If you show up for work and take a casual attitude to the tasks requested, if you do not show almost as much seriousness or purposefulness as your boss, why would you expect to be taken seriously? Approaching work with a casual attitude will not enable you to be 30% more valuable in twenty-four months.

If you had $100,000 in chips in play at a blackjack table, do you think you could pay close attention to the game for a couple hours at a time? You do. A lack of seriousness may lead to the economy taking all your chips in its next sweep of layoffs.

3. Humble Confidence

Humility is one of the most elusive of human traits. Try to describe it. It has an ethereal quality to it that makes it hard to pin down. People say they value humility, yet we all know that other people are attracted to confidence. We need to believe in ourselves, we need to speak and act with confidence, or people will see you as weak. But if you are too confident you get labeled as cocky or arrogant and the now-dated "not a team player."

Humble Confidence makes you bold in what you know and still open to feedback and ideas that will make your work stronger. People find humility endearing and it makes others want to help and support you. Confidence inspires and makes other people want to follow you. One without the other can be lopsided. Confident people say, "Let's approach it this way." Humble Confident people add, "but I am open to other suggestions if anyone has one." Confident people welcome an argument and enjoy shopping in the marketplace of ideas. Humble Confident people ask other people to put their positions forward and distribute the credit.

4. Personal Objectivity

So far this book has advised you to be relentlessly original and Pre-Empowered and here I am suggesting that you have to do it in a way that does not make it seem like "it's all about me." People will dig in against you if they think it's about you. They will illogically hope for you to fail to teach you a lesson if they think it's about what you want, even though you work in the same company or group.

Objectivity helps you put some distance between what you the individual are doing and what you are doing as a function of your role and your objectives. Low-ego, high performers attract others to their causes and build relationships. Objectivity helps you shift from opinions and personalities to facts and data. It will also help you avoid getting emotional when the defensiveness builds and the situation simmers.

Toughness is another quality people want to see in their staff. You should be hardworking, resilient and resourceful. However, no one likes to work with someone who is pigheaded and stubborn, who proves over and over again that they do not listen. Some people are too competitive and never want to lose a hand no matter how trivial.

Don't have a stake in one particular approach until the facts suggest it is likely to work better than another. Avoid arguments by stating: "Let's test it," or, "Let's see what the numbers say." Don't act like you have something to prove personally, act on what you can prove operationally.

5. Tune Your Antenna

When you talk in business, what percent of your energy is focused on keeping a coherent train of thought and for making a strong point? 90%? More? As you concentrate, do you break eye contact and use bridging words like "so," "and," or "well," to keep control of the topic and drive your point home? Do you know exactly why you are talking?

Some primary reasons to speak are to:
- Deliver an update
- Answer a question
- Sell an idea or build buy-in
- Generate discussion
- Build a relationship

Each of these reasons has an interactive component that requires you to stop broadcasting and Tune Your Antenna every few minutes to the listeners to see what they are broadcasting back. Are they agreeing or disagreeing? How is their body language? Do they want to interject? Tuning Your Antenna requires you to watch their eyes and face and body posture. Stop speaking and leave openings for them to broadcast. Even better, ask open-ended questions like, "How do you see it?" or, "What are your thoughts on it?" You will not know if you are achieving your speaking objectives without Tuning Your Antenna to pick up the signal they are broadcasting back.

6. Ignorant Optimism

Sometimes we approach problems without a lot of knowledge of them or the solutions that have been considered already. People who have tried to fix a problem and given up or failed have a vested interest in seeing you fail at it too because your success will highlight their prior failure. This is one of the reasons companies hire steep Angle of Ascent people but often wait until it is too late to do it.

Ignorant Optimism will allow you to consider new approaches and one of these might be a breakthrough. Some of the polite ways to get the dissenters out of the way are to ask: Do you have a post-mortem write up of your findings? Are you 100% confident the tracking was correct and that it failed? Were the findings statistically significant? Add: maybe it wasn't the right time then and we should try it again now.

7. Learning Zone

If you accept the premise that practice trumps talent, you will find more motivation to develop yourself. You have heard of the comfort zone, where people generate a sense of comfort and confidence by doing things they have done before and mastered. In order to grow every week of every year, you have to work in the rigor of the Learning Zone. In the Learning Zone you stretch yourself a few percent beyond your current capabilities. The challenge and accomplishment generates stronger confidence and satisfaction than operating in the comfort zone.

8. Failure Absorbance

> "I have not failed 700 times. I have not failed once. I have succeeded in proving that those 700 ways will not work. When I have eliminated the ways that will not work, [it is easier to] find the way that will work."

This Thomas Edison quote about the development of an effective light bulb filament brackets the extreme of Failure Absorbance. When you see failure as a component of success, it will cease to frighten and deter you. You will be more comfortable experimenting and managing through it. Failure builds character and humility; people will respect your perseverance.

How many times should you try making something succeed before moving on? Three to five experiments will provide you more data and knowledge of the topic than most other people have, and even if the experiment doesn't prove out, the attempts will likely inform other thought processes and new experiments to try.

Do you quit at blackjack if you lose two hands in a row? Why would you quit at work after losing once or twice? Because in blackjack you don't get paid if you don't bet, but in business you continue to get paid even when you stop betting. Keep trying.

9. Problem Obliteration

Without problems work would be boring. The harder the problems are to solve, the more important and better paid the people who solve them.

In your first weeks in a new job, you will see it with fresh eyes and the problems will be obvious. Write them down. Over time you will get busier and will get used to the problems. Like a squeak in the floor, you know where it is and can usually step around it without making the noise. You have to recognize a problem and get some agreement on it before it can be solved.

You'll notice people on your team complaining about the same issues. If one person sees it, it may be them. If everyone sees it, it has wheels. However, problems left unresolved lead to mistakes and mistakes over time lead to layoffs. So, obliterate problems. Don't go around. Don't go over. Don't mask them. Obliterate them. Problems come from many sources, but they are maintained by ignorance or neglect. Most problems can be addressed and initial solutions put in place in two hours or less.

10. Bridge Building

Relationships are crucially important in business and personal life, but I did not include them as a fundamental skill because you cannot practice them in the abstract by yourself but have to practice them in context with other people.

Bridge Building connects you to people who can help drive success. You should reach up to mentors, out to peers, and down to junior colleagues as their mentor. Ask good questions, listen to the answers, remember the information or jot it down.

> A friend said that people are like corks, if you don't weigh them down their natural happiness will float them up. I see Bridge Building the same way. If we unburden ourselves from our biases and assumptions, we can build bridges with people without much effort. It's natural.

In the final section of this book we will dive deeper into a few of the discussed topics – like expanding on the idea of fortifying yourself with strong peers – and introduce a few new ones, such as cadence, risk management, and culture. I will reflect candidly on decades worth of workplace experiences and speak specifically on the takeaway points from successes and failures.

IV. MANAGING YOUR CAREER

19. Cadence

Cadence is a popular topic in business right now. You will hear senior management mention it often when discussing planning. Cadence encompasses the following three concepts:
1. Tactics
2. Frequency
3. Predictability

Cadence refers to tangible tactical output, like software releases, outbound calls, new creative, A/B tests, site updates, and content published. It does not include strategic planning, plan revision, process definition and informational analysis. It does not include ad hoc and one-off activity, only activity that can be replicated.

Frequency defines the speed of tactical output per time period without which there will be no cadence. So whatever tactical effort is planned at a frequency, it must be resourced correctly for sustained output without the heroic efforts and sacrifice that sometimes come with major projects.

Tactics at a reliable frequency make planning and forecasting more accurate. Making a business grow reliably is the primary objective of senior management.

At one company I worked for, we wanted to hire a new PR agency to help us drive a content-led strategy and build thought leadership. Each agency we interviewed told us they totally supported the idea and were so excited to work with us because we "really got it." All the agencies pitched a good content story, but my boss and I became obsessed with what frequency of blog and social posts would be required to drive traffic and leads with content because we knew we had no capacity to write it. As we zeroed in on the cadence, the agencies became more evasive and gave answers like, "It depends," or they would advise and guide and cooperate to help promote and amplify the content we created. We did not need an agency to tell us to write, that was the tactical output we wanted to hire. We had neither a full-time PR person nor a full-time writer, so we asked this question: Assume we will produce nothing but only answer your questions and provide guidance, what cadence of content production will you produce within the $15k retainer? Some said zero and were quickly eliminated. The winner gave a realistic number and signed up for the cadence of content output. The cadence of their proposal allowed us to imagine the partnership and make a plan and forecast.

At another job we decided to determine the cadence of blog posting as a primary goal and raised it from one a week to seven. There were a lot of complaints about quality and thin content and I was threatened with the possibility of a penalty from Google. We did as many as seven posts and often did five. We saw many benefits from the active and robust blog and twenty-four people within the company wrote for it. Starting with the cadence and working backward made it much easier to plan the editorial calendar and schedule the work.

Build cadence into your planning and output and watch how positively other departments and senior management respond.

Further, building cadence can help temper risk, a subject to focus on next.

20. Risk Management

"Success has many fathers, but failure is an orphan." – Unknown

Risk and reward in corporations do not correlate correctly. Rather than 1:1, I guess it is 3:1, meaning that three units of risk will yield only one unit of gain. Mistakes are afforded more weight than successes, and that damage to the formula makes people in corporations careful, conservative, and political. In poker, you do not even call a bet unless you think your pot payout and odds of winning the hand are even or better.

One of the best ways to maintain a steep angle of ascent is to not go backwards professionally, personally, or interpersonally. Ironically, people expect others to show a normal level of self-preservation and take only reasonable risks. Your desire for self-preservation relieves other people of careful scrutiny of your motivations and movements. If you are so committed to your issue that you will sacrifice your personal security to achieve it, in a corporation it will generate not respect but suspicion because your behavior does not make immediate sense. Others will look for an ulterior motive or scheme. They will trust you less and they will avoid you for fear of you damaging their brand within the company. Sadly, they might even root for your failure for the same reason people like to look at car accident scenes: other people's failure accentuates our own lack of failure. I know. This chapter is depressing.

The biggest career setback is getting fired for cause. There are two main reasons people get fired: inadequate competence and unpleasantness. To avoid the first, do not bluff your way into a job that is over your head and never stop improving your hard skills and job knowledge. Unpleasantness is even easier to avoid than lack of skills. Make your comportment professional and considerate and appear to focus on the company's goals more than your own. Do not care so much about a particular item that you take poor personal and professional risks to get it done. Put it back in context: is this item critical to the company? Is there a lot of money at stake? Will it matter in three months or nine months? If not, keep your risk-taking efforts and passion in balance with the importance of the project or task.

Years ago I was working a partner program with a large PC manufacturer and we were going to do a joint press release. I asked a PR manager to help with plenty of time in the schedule. After a few weeks with little movement, the date started getting closer and I began to press harder. Then she told me another project was taking priority and that she would not be able to work on it for a while. With the deadline approaching, I started dialing up the tone of my emails. I escalated directly to her boss. Then my boss decided that we did not need to do the release. Needless to say, I became her least favorite colleague and she never helped on any future requests. Ten years later I ran into her and we were having a very pleasant conversation and catching up and she said, "Didn't we work together on some urgent partner release that didn't turn out right?" I had mostly forgotten. She hadn't.

Other people, especially those who do not know us that well, remember the little things we do wrong and few or none of the little or even medium-sized things we do right. Don't spend your personal capital on small issues and fewer people will find you unpleasant.

When you are considering something you think professionally or personally risky, run through the following questions:

1. What would a conversation on this issue with your boss or HR be like?

2. What would a conversation on this issue with your spouse, kids, or parents be like?
3. What if your decision and actions on this issue were printed in the newspaper? How would the article read?
4. What could go wrong? How wrong could it go? Is that risk reasonable given the gain?

If you know that you generally have a risk tolerance higher than other people, then use alternate decision processes from what you normally do. If you are emotionally driven, use paper and pen to list out facts and review. Check that your emotions are not trying to short-circuit your thought processes with justifications. If you are intuitively driven, try consulting with two people before you engage your issue.

Additionally, you should not take a job working for a boss that you do not fit with. Check your gut during interviews and conversations. Do you have a queasy or uneasy feeling? Is your mind starting to paper over potential problems because your mind wants the relief of getting a job, any job? Ask other interviewers what kind of a boss the person is. Try to check around with other people who may have worked with that person in the past.

Filtering
Social interaction requires each of us to modify our behavior to fit the norms of the groups we interact with. Socially effective people look for the median behavior and regress towards it. Most people see the

benefit of acknowledging the enormity of the human ego and the priority and subjectivity of people's feelings. People are not usually rational; most of their decisions are driven by their feelings, and that is why people are very careful with what they say. That is also why people are so cautious about speaking up and offering opinions. It is easier to offend or upset another person by saying something than there is a downside risk for keeping quiet. Personally, I find people who hold their opinions tighter than those around them to be selfish and self-serving. They prioritize their security over the problem at hand.

After working for more than twenty years, I realized how critical this filtering is, and as I started to filter more I started to do better with people. As a young person, I filtered and held back maybe 10% of my reactions, and I got tangled up with people often. I kept adjusting my assessment of how important relationships and filtering are relative to work quality and productivity. I used to think it was 20% relationships and 80% work, and each time I failed with people, I adjusted up the relationship weight. As the filtering rate goes higher, I am not sure a company can maintain enough talent and productivity to succeed. Companies need excellent salespeople, creative designers, talented coders, operations experts, and analysts. Talent and productivity should trump overly-developed internal people skills for the best of those types of employees.

So if people skills are 60% of success in a group or organization, understanding what makes people skills good is critical. The basic skill is not saying the wrong thing at the wrong time and the technique for that is filtering. As I said, I used to filter only 10% of my reactions, then I raised it to 20% and life got easier, I raised it to 30% and started to let problems I saw in other people's work slide and incubate until other people saw them and had to deal with them. I was so proud of myself; I was taking less risk, doing less work, and getting along better with people. I thought I had found the answer, the secret formula. One problem was that our overall readiness and success rate seemed to be slipping also. Over time, I wanted to know how other people filtered.

> I started to ask other people how much they filtered in social situations with more than eight people and no alcohol, expecting them to confirm the 20-30% number I had found. Instead I heard numbers like 60%, 70%, and even 100%. When someone told me 100% filtering, I blurted out, "Well, doesn't that make you a phony and a manipulator? Doesn't that mean everything you say to people including me is not genuine?" Oops! There I go again. He was in sales and he explained to me that he was in the business of building relationships and matching stories. He said that before every meeting he thinks carefully about what he will say and what the other person might say and mostly sticks to that script in his head. I was shocked, but I respected his approach to his relationship-based selling.

It is hard to be prescriptive on this topic, but if you work in an environment that requires people to filter more than half of their reactions and opinions, I suspect the company is not healthy, is rather political, and will eventually lose to a company that doesn't waste time and energy padding every interaction with bull and ego dust. Ask people you know at healthy, fast-growing companies and they will probably tell you that people are rather frank and open. If employees are holding back half their input and value, they are wasting half the company's most valuable and expensive resource. Choose to work in a company that rewards people who speak up and contribute and fires the ones who hold back and scheme. Rather than using a heavy filter, consider: What impact will your plan or comment have on other people? What will their reaction be? Consult the people who might be impacted first and get input. Ask them for permission, even if you don't need it, as it will increase their sense of control and their trust in you. Try to never surprise people with your comments, especially in large groups or in front of their boss. These more refined filtering tactics should help protect your relationships while also advancing company progress.

"It Depends" or I'm Answering in a Politically Advantageous Way

"It depends" is an intellectually bereft answer, so why do people use it so often? Reasons include: they don't know an answer, they know but don't want to give an opinion, they are worried about being wrong, they don't want to take a position because they worry that the questioner is trying to corner them, or they don't want to disagree or argue because they believe getting along is more important than getting it right. Those are a lot of reasons that can compromise the company or the group and protect the individual using it in the short-term.

People ask questions for a few primary reasons: they want to know the answer, they want to test the knowledge and skill of a person, or they want to make another person talk so they do not have to. "It depends" will not satisfy any of these needs. Intelligent people know that situations in life and business are not completely uniform and therefore reactions to issues need to be adjusted to the context in which they are found. If you say, "it depends," you will force the other person to say, "on what?" or, "give me a range." Intelligent people know the difference between a fact and an estimate. "It depends" is a cop-out that blows your credibility as a subject-matter expert or thought leader.

Intelligent, confident, experienced people give qualified responses. To ensure that no one thinks you are saying an answer will be irrevocably accurate in every situation for eternity, make it an informed projection with:

"I would estimate…"

"In my experience…"

"I have seen it work or fail in these cases…"

"On average…"

"Let me answer by providing an example…"

You can also bluff an answer that you do not have experience or information about, which is sometimes done, but the credibility downside of bluffing is obvious.

If you suspect someone will give you "it depends," ask a qualified question: "How long did this take the last time you did this?" "How much did it cost the last client who did this?" "How many people did it take on average across the last three projects?"

And if you really don't know and don't have a decent guess, you can say so and specify a time when you will come back with the answer, but do not use this too often as it implies a lack of experience and subject matter expertise.

It's not hard to find examples of "it depends" as it comes up so often. Last time I heard it, a lawyer at a company said, "Let me answer like a lawyer and say 'it depends.'" And let me listen like a five-year-old and tune out as soon as you say, "Let me answer like a lawyer," and throw in an award for the worst setup line of the year. Might as well say, "Not gonna answer your question, tough."

21. Leadership, Management & Influence

Leadership: setting direction and motivating people to get there.
Management: developing the processes, tools and tactics to get
work done.
Influence: the innate and learned skill of getting people to do what
you believe needs to be done.

Interestingly, none of these three skills requires a title
to implement, but leadership and management become
easier with a title because others expect leadership and
management directions from people with certain titles.
Of the three, influence is the most important, the most
valuable, and the most available to people at every level
of an organization. People without higher titles often
feel frustrated by their lack of influence, and they aspire
to have authority but are unaware of the responsibility
that comes with it. They wonder how they can get
people to do the desired work without the leverage of
reporting lines and the power to reprimand or fire.

Influence is strengthened by preparation, listening,
speaking, and by building agreement, credibility, and
accountability.

A few hours of preparation will usually enhance
your influence between you and the people you will try
to persuade. Facts, agendas, discussion documents,
clear meeting requests, and confirmation that the right
people will attend a discussion all reduce diffusion of
influence and momentum.

People might overlook the power of listening as
they try to influence others and rely too much on

speaking. Listening validates the speakers, and people like others who validate them best. People are more likely to follow people they like.

Building agreement combines listening, speaking, and drawing all members of the group into a discussion of appropriate intensity. A certain level of democratic intensity will give people a greater feeling of comfort in moving forward even if they are not completely clear on the details. Actual voting and scoring towards the end of the discussion will identify people who do not agree and allow you to address their concerns. Failure to address their concerns will lead to diffusion of influence or outright sabotage later.

Credibility is the most important component of influence. It combines your subject matter expertise, preparation, and prior track record of accuracy in making decisions and predicting outcomes. Think about what predicting outcomes means; it means you can predict the future. If more than ¾ of your decisions and predictions prove accurate, your credibility and influence will be strong. Establishing your credibility track record requires you to make your opinions known before execution and results. People who say nothing do not run the risk of being wrong, but they also do not run the risk of becoming much more influential. So do your homework, listen to the options, do some more homework, and cast your vote in public or in writing to your boss. Being right builds your credibility, but people who were loudly wrong will also resent you for it. Watch out for and avoid the traps they will set for you to bring your "score" down to theirs.

Lastly, influence requires you to hold yourself and others accountable for commitments. If people miss a deliverable, talk to them directly about it, remind them of their commitment, and explain what the impact of missing the deliverable has on your project. If missing recurs, politely escalate the matter and keep the pressure on. Excuses destroy your credibility; you might as well say, "I am not capable or influential enough to get the job done because people do not respect me and I am an ineffective communicator." Alternatives to excuses include apologies followed by quick action, alternative solutions, and escalations. Never utter excuses and never accept them.

Hacker Profile Five - Riki

Education: BS University of California at Davis, 3.3 GPA. Worked part-time in college and practiced Brazilian Jiu Jitsu for 3 years and won a regional championship and state bronze in his first year.

Parents paid for college with Riki agreeing to repay 10%.

Background: Parents are still married, stable upper-middle-class family, father is a VP of Marketing, mother works in a supermarket. Has 1 younger brother.

Progress: Riki is in the 5th year of his career. He has been promoted 6 times, changed companies three times, and quintupled his starting salary. By the chart on page 13 in the 10% column he is projected to make over $500,000 in salary and commission before age 35.

Riki has been an active musician since he was 10 and spends much of his free time drumming and performing for an alternative rock band. Riki listens to 20+ non-fiction audio books per year on his commute.

Riki is a gifted writer and an extremely articulate speaker. He self-published his first novel at the age of 21 and writes and produces music. He hosted a regular podcast called The Wealthy Healthy.

He is already a technical subject matter expert in his field and was awarded **the** 2017 Next Big Rising Star by the San Francisco Bay Area Innovation Group.

He is below average height.

Riki was offered a VP of Digital and Sales Strategy job before the age of 25. He ended up declining it.

Riki was exposed to the key ideas in Talent Is Overrated and the 10,000 hours of deliberate practice ideas in Peak, Outliers, and Grit before he graduated college.

Keys to success: totally coachable, learns easily from other people's advice and their mistakes. Able to understand others and invests time to make clever plans to maneuver around and through them. Rarely makes mistakes.

Last pertinent details are that he is my son, and he was the editor of this book when he was 20.

22. Crew

Most people understand and appreciate the importance of personal network when looking for jobs, especially to help open doors at big companies.

According to John Bennett of Queens University of Charlotte, "Research tells us that between 60-80% of jobs are found through personal relationships."

In my career, personal connections helped me get 65% of my jobs, just as the stat above predicts. Within startups there is a network that is significantly more important than personal connections; I call this "Crew." In my experience, more than a third of startups are run by people who not only know each other but have also worked together before. Crew is the team of people who work together and develop loyalty and thus try to work together again and again. That makes securing a startup job without a Crew connection even more difficult.

Crew is any two or more people who work well together, trust each other, and who decide in successive companies to choose each other again. In startups people expect it, and if you are a boss who cannot recruit your old crew, people will wonder why not. It means you are not a leader people want to follow. Approach Crew like this:

Select a good boss. In the interview be honest with yourself about whether you respect that person and can be loyal. Sometimes you really need the job and cannot afford to start applying somewhere else. Remember to

133

ask other people in the interview team about your prospective manager's management style. What kinds of people complement him/her? What kinds of people clash?

Don't hire a boss who might get fired or leave soon. If your boss leaves or gets cut, you might have three bosses in one year: the original boss, an interim boss, and the permanent new boss. Odds are that the second and the third bosses will care less about you than the original boss. Existing management often lays off existing people just before the new boss arrives, so the new boss does not have to. New bosses usually bring in their own Crew, so they will often make it impossible for you to succeed, to connect with them, or they may just outright fire you to bring in their own people.

Like the boss you selected. If you do not like your boss, guess what? Your boss almost certainly does not like you. So, decide if you can get to really like your boss and be authentically loyal, and if not, look for a new boss. Before you change companies, see if you can find a new boss within your company. Don't waste years of your career clinging to a job with a boss whose Crew you cannot join.

Pick your people carefully. Bosses need Crew almost as much as staff does. Pick employees who exhibit an awareness of and focus on the codependent and bilateral relationships between boss and staff. Oftentimes you inherit people who are loyal to the old boss and resentful of you as the new boss. Try to win them over by investing time and energy in their personal development and advancement. Everyone has a soft spot for a person who will help him/her climb the ladder.

Exhibit loyalty. Listen, follow instructions, be transparent, be honest, be helpful; put the needs of the person you are loyal to before your own.

Pick executives with good reputations in the business community and ones who have more companies in their future. Look for fast trackers and serial entrepreneurs and stick with them. I call this finding your CEO, which I will explain momentarily. Rather than getting a master's degree, invest a thousand hours of your life meeting quality business people with a special focus on finding an executive, visionary or serial entrepreneur whom you respect greatly. When you identify this person, find a way to hook to them and become part of their Crew. The phrase comes from something I was telling my sons about how to join the workforce in Silicon Valley. "Get out there and find your CEO."

I know a man who is that high-quality, successful CEO; my sons know him and they do not doubt his ability. The fact that everyone I know who knows him thinks highly of him makes it easy to conclude that he is indeed my CEO. After a bad outing with my old "James" friend, I realized that I had found my CEO, but I had not yet taken my own advice and connected my career with his. A lunch and a dinner later I interviewed with his team, and I started working for him as his senior director of marketing.

Finding Your Crew Boss

As mentioned, when I eventually came to the realization that I wanted to work for someone I knew and believed in – my CEO – I took my own advice and was happier than I have ever been at work.

In order to find a leader you can believe in and stake your livelihood on, you should identify in them the following:

1. An idea for a service or product
2. An ability to sell the idea to investors and consumers
3. Dogged persistence
4. Drive to win
5. Tendency to build others up and make them strong
6. Overflowing energy
7. A desire to share gains instead of hoard them

Let's get specific about this tactic and how to increase your chances of finding one. For starters, look at the people you do business with and if you think one of the leaders of one of those companies is a high-quality person, ask your sales rep to set up a meeting and connect directly. Join clubs, industry groups, professional clubs, skills development classes and clubs, start-up clubs, go to meet ups. Listen closely to people you know and if they talk about someone they know with admiration or reverence. Finding strong people is your first step. The second step is connecting with them. You can ask them for an informational meeting to get some advice, invite them out for breakfast, a coffee, or lunch. You could offer to bring them lunch, so you can have a quick working lunch in their office and save them time. If you do a sport and they do the same one, you can invite them for a round of golf, a game of tennis, go for a run, or a bike ride, if that's what they do. You can invite them to a ball game or a show. You can join their gym and work out with them. I started a monthly wine club that has been running for over ten years, and it allows me an easy and flexible way to connect with people I meet as most people drink wine and most successful people enjoy socializing. One man I met was and still is the CEO of a software company whose product I licensed. We kept in touch and became closer in the wine club I run.

One important aspect of this advice is that in order to join the management team with this person and potentially get rich, you need to identify them and place your bet before their company is large enough to attract top-tier talent from the market at large. That means you need to keep your radar up and be a great judge of character and potential, like a VC, but you will invest your years instead of money. In truth, finding a successful CEO with a great personality in the first year or two of their enterprise will be difficult. What if you find that person, but the enterprise is already mature and already has the whole management team in place?

Is it worth it to take a middle management position? Yes. This will provide a decent opportunity, but it will not likely be one that will make you wealthy.

1 in 10 startups make it to profitability. 1 in 11 profitable startups make it to a valuation over $100,000,000. That works out to 1 in 110 startups that can provide you $1 million if you own 1%. Most people will not be able to connect with a CEO or president and join that management team, so does this advice translate to finding a boss and developing a very strong working relationship so that you are on their Crew and do not have to interview in the open market? Yes, it does. A good mentor and boss who works for an excellent CEO is better than a good mentor and boss who works for a mediocre one. Watch and listen for an executive who is good at picking winning companies and winning CEOs. Listen for that admiration and loyalty and narrow your search to people whom others believe is their best-choice CEO.

Next, I will discuss how culture influences and ultimately permeates into every aspect of a company, making it a high-value opportunity for companies and individuals entering companies.

23. Culture

Corporate Culture defines how close or far from 100% emotional and mental contribution a company engenders from its employees-- how engaged, bold, confident, and passionate they act in private and in public to drive company success.

The most important drivers of engagement are power and trust. The more a company distributes power and communicates trust, the more responsible employees will feel and behave. Positive culture also requires individuality, alignment, trust, transparency, respect, and employee security. They will fuel additional sustained originality and organic momentum that a company cannot drive with monetary compensation.

Culture guides how groups of people think and act when no one is actively managing. The norms of behavior and interaction are defined by its leaders and enforced by its senior members. Culture defines how success is measured and what is valued most.

In the Mormon culture, community, tithing, service, the mission to evangelize, and not drinking alcohol and caffeine are all commonly observed. In exchange for observance, members get included in a close-knit community that will provide social and emotional support, help in times of need, and assist with starting and succeeding in business.

In Washington DC the culture of partisanship and corruption has led to gridlock and an ineffective federal system. Elected representatives put party before district, state, and national interest. They show the most loyalty to large donors in their own bid for reelection. Political fighting, grandstanding, smear tactics, and self-promotion are the norms. They refer to it as blood sport. Congress is enjoying its lowest approval rating in history.

On Wall Street the culture of greed drives behavior. Highly intelligent people use their knowledge and skills to find short-term opportunity and advantage as they challenge and cross the boundaries of the law and morality. Many will do anything for a million dollars, even if it costs someone else two million or the economy ten million. Only 30% of Americans have a positive view of the banking industry.

Netflix explained that its culture is based on high performance, transparency, and freedom & responsibility in an environment that is well aligned and loosely coupled. They trust people to make decisions and hold them accountable for more than one mistake. In other words, they will readily remove them from the culture after the second mistake.

At one company I worked, the culture was not explicitly documented, but as we interviewed we defined culture fit as people who: care a lot about what they do, have a thirst for knowledge and a growth mindset, are driven and competitive, and are willing to step on some toes to help the company succeed. We understood that people with these traits are likely more emotional and harder in some ways to manage, but we thought that was a fair trade-off to optimize for in our goalset.

The United States Marines explain their culture this way:

> The core values of the Marines, honor, courage and commitment, define how every Marine in the Corps thinks, acts, and fights. Throughout the battlefields of the 21st Century, every Marine in the Corps must be confident they can rely on each other to think, act, and lead. In the chaos of battle, character matters.

The Marines' culture presents quite a contrast to Washington and Wall Street.

In the absence of a clearly defined and supported culture, an ambiguous and amorphous culture will fill the gap. Ambiguity weakens the cohesion of the group as member expectations, thoughts, and actions diverge, sap spirit, and waste resources. Political behavior and conflicts are more likely and conflict resolution becomes more difficult. Ambiguity will reduce individual decisiveness, confidence, passion, and performance and lead to frustration. Ambiguity concentrates influence at the top; clarity distributes influence to the edges.

People are social creatures and prefer to be part of a group, to like the people they spend time with, and to share in the group's identity. With a clear culture, people can plan, prioritize, and make trade-offs and generate less friction and fewer conflicts with other members. A clear culture attracts the right people to join. A clear culture empowers people to decide and act with less fear of taking action.

To define a culture in a company, start with core values. Most companies select three to five. The leader needs to build consensus around these values with the management team. If any of the management team do not or cannot exemplify the values, they need to be removed. The leader should communicate the values to the wider team. Then all senior members should use the values to hire, fire, mentor, evaluate, promote, and compensate members. Talk the talk and walk the walk.

One of the reinforcements of a strong culture is delineation and differentiation from other ones. Ben Horowitz calls this a cultural design point and gives three examples:

> Amazon used to make desks out of doors to show they cared about saving money.

> Andreesen Horrowitz charges partners $10 a minute for being late to meetings with entrepreneurs to show respect.

> Mark Zuckerberg encouraged employees to move fast and break things to enable risk taking.

Cultural design points help make the core values more intelligible, especially to new members.

Operationally, the company must set annual and quarterly plans and must review performance against it at set periods. When objectives are missed, countermeasures must be considered and implemented. Vision statements and mission statements are more closely related to the operating plan than the culture. Fun activities, events, and perks should be used as tactics to increase employee retention, but they should not be confused with or exchanged with defining and nurturing a clear, high-performance culture.

A company with an unpleasant but clear culture can still be successful, but one with an ambiguous one almost certainly cannot.

At a recent job we came up with the analogy of renters and owners to describe 2 approaches to the job. Renters do the minimum and rarely invest in improving their place or neighborhood; owners go the extra mile and look for ways to improve their unit and naturally make the neighborhood a better place to live. Renters are complacent; owners are proactive. Renters complain; owners are optimistic and provide solutions. Renters take benefits for granted; owners appreciate and show appreciation more. If a company attracts too many renters and fails to "evict" them they will bring down teams, departments, divisions and eventually the whole company.

However, management can unwittingly foster renters by dehumanizing residents, undermining motivation with overly tactical playbooks, and by not supporting an open and transparent neighborhood where residents are given a chance to ask questions and give input on important issues. The most mature employees will find a way to behave like owners and deliver value despite management's unintended hindrance.

Culture is probably one of the top three most important factors for a company's success. If you are a manager, use culture to enhance the performance of employees. If you are an employee, explore and understand the culture before you join a company and embrace the culture while you work there. If you find yourself fighting the culture, then find a company with a better-fitting culture for you.

24. Corporate Maturity and Its Opposite

So, you have reviewed my premise, observations, insights, and anecdotes. Are you convinced that corporate maturity is the key quality that drives promotion?

If you are not yet convinced, look at the opposite situation from promotion—getting fired. What are the main reasons people get fired? One, they lack the skill to do the job, or operational maturity. Two, they do not get along well with people, do not communicate well, are not well liked, and have weak and broken relationships, or lack relationship maturity. Three, they get too emotional, over-react and make other people uncomfortable, or lack emotional maturity. Four, they learn and grow slowly, are hard to train, have bad judgment, and have trouble understanding and solving problems, or lack mental maturity.

Think about what promotion entails: elevating the responsibility, authority, and status of a person. Those who grant the promotion are looking for people who have proven themselves ready to succeed at the next level. Maturity is nearly synonymous with advancement and readiness.

Let's review the hacks in this book that support that accelerated corporate maturity in the four primary forms.

Mental maturity hacks:
- Deliberate practice
- Feedback attraction
- Pre-empowerment
- Goalset optimization
- Learning zone
- Be an expert and evolve your knowledge
- Intellectual toughness
- Idea attentiveness
- Ignorant optimism

Emotional maturity hacks:
- Credibility and trust
- Double your luck
- Memorably positive
- Robust joy
- Leadership, management & influence
- Professional seriousness
- Coachability
- Humble confidence
- Personal objectivity
- Failure absorbance

Relationship maturity hacks:
- Managing up
- Managing laterally
- Managing down
- Fortification
- Start with yes
- Crew
- Tune your antenna
- Bridge building

Operational maturity hacks:
- Remember by doing
- Source of delay
- Aim for ten times more
- Cadence
- Risk management
- Culture
- Problem obliteration

The above is a summary of 34 fast track hacks any 2 or 3 of which, if you are missing them, could unlock the key to higher levels of corporate maturity and your next promotion.

Hacker Profile 6 – Laura

Education: BS University of California at Berkeley with a double major in Statistics and French Literature.

Background: Parents are still married, stable upper-middle-class family, father is a financial adviser and mother is an actuary. Has 2 younger sisters.

Parents paid for college. Laura worked 30 and 40 hours a week in final two years of college.

Completed 4 internships in college, and she ended up working full time at one of them.

Played classical piano from age 5 and played violin in middle school and high school.

Laura competed in track and cross country in high school and ran cross country in college.

Was a member of the Daily Californian newspaper, competed in Model United Nations, and was a member of the CAL Actuarial League.

Progress: Laura is in the 3rd year of her career and has been promoted 4 times and is now a growth marketing leader in a venture-funded startup.

Keys to success: Extremely high energy, organization, boldness, and ability to deliver work at rapid speed.

Laura reads 24 books per year.

HACKER PROFILES: Fast Track Hacker Composite Profile

The six hackers researched make a great sample because none of them had the typical advantages people associate with success: money, connections, the best prep and private schools, and excess height.

Of the 6 of them, none of their parents divorced. I believe this is conducive to stability, stronger relationships, communication, and development. I believe divorce usually stunts development and maturity. It can have the opposite also.

6 of the 6 have brothers and sisters. 5 of 6 of them have younger siblings. I think this on average increases maturity and sense of responsibility. People with siblings have far more social development opportunities than only-children.

All 6 are well below average height, which may have increased their drive and effort. None of them are from wealthy families. Most did not have noteworthy connections to help them get opportunities.

All 6 are very lean. Being lean can counterbalance a lack of height and has positive associations with exercise and self-discipline. You can control your height to a degree by standing and sitting up straight, but you have almost complete ability to stay lean with diet and exercise.

All 6 are good looking and dress appropriately. While you cannot control exactly what you look like, you should make the most of what you have.

All 6 of them did internships in their field before graduation.

6 of 6 went to public school through high school. 5 of 6 went to public universities. None of the 6 had an A average in college. 5 of 6 played team sports in high school. 3 were competitive athletes in college.

3 of them earned BSs and 3 earned BAs. All 6 graduated in 4 or 3 years. 5 of the 6 did not get graduate degrees. 5 of 6 started working in their field right out of college. This supports my belief that graduate school is usually not worth the extra investment and can slow you down.

All 6 are very approachable and make time to connect with people. All 6 are persuasive and even compelling. 5 of the 6 speak with a very loud voice.

Probably the most relevant common element is how much they worked in college and what kind of work they did. Jennifer, Mark, Ryan, and Laura all worked close to full time, 40 hours a week, while maintaining solid grades. Mike and Riki worked 20 hours a week.

5 of 6 now read multiple times more non-fiction than the people around them.

All 6 had parents who did not spoil them and 4 of the 6 had some economic deprivation that appears to have increased their motivation.

6 of 6 have very high energy, are extremely good communicators who reliably return messages quickly, and have a positive or solutions view on almost every situation.

Conclusion

Each of the traits and characteristics in the hacker profile above shaves some number of months or years off the time it takes to make it to vice president in a corporation. The profile, approach, and style are why 2 of them made vice president before they were 33 and one was offered before he was 25. Anyone of any background can learn from them and what they did to Hack the Corporate Fast Track.

Do I think that people from wealthy families who go to top private schools will not achieve success? Of course not, those people are talented, hard working, and often geniuses. Another way onto the corporate fast track exists and is available to almost everyone who learns these unwritten rules to accelerate corporate maturity.

Dave Lawson, who came up with the title for the book, asked me if some principles in the book were most critical to avoiding failure. My top failure avoidance items are: Start With Yes, Memorably Positive, Filtering, Be Easy to Manage, and Managing Up.

If I could go back in time, I would spend my hour a week reading and practicing this book. I would score myself on the traits and skills. Each week I would focus solidly on one of the topics or sections. I would find mentors or colleagues who could provide feedback on my performance and progress. I would read and internalize a minimum of 10 business books per year.

I would use this inside knowledge to Hack the Corporate Fast Track. Will you?

Erik Newton www.linkedin.com/in/eriknewton

Worksheets

5 Hacker Traits to Work On and 1 to 100 Self-Evaluation Scores
1.   _____
2.   _____
3.   _____
4.   _____
5.   _____

Plans for Working on Those 5 Traits
1.
2.
3.
4.
5.

People to Emulate
1.
2.
3.

People to Mentor Me and Provide Feedback
1.
2.
3.

Date for Check-In Evaluation

5 More Hacker Traits to Work On and 1 to 100 Self-Evaluation Scores

1. _____
2. _____
3. _____
4. _____
5. _____

Plans for Working on Those 5 Traits

1.
2.
3.
4.
5.

People to Emulate

1.
2.
3.

People to Mentor Me and Provide Feedback

1.
2.
3.

Date for Check-In Evaluation

Bibliography and Recommended Reading List

Talent Is Overrated by Geoff Colvin

Influence: The Psychology of Persuasion by Robert Cialdini

Pre-suasion by Robert Cialdini

Drive by Daniel Pink

The 48 Laws of Power by Robert Greene

Linchpin by Seth Godin

Tribes by Seth Godin

Never Split the Difference by Chris Voss

Play Bigger by Al Ramadan

The Unwritten Laws of Business by W. J. King

Outliers by Malcolm Gladwell

Blink by Malcolm Gladwell

The Hard Thing About Hard Things by Ben Horowitz

The 10X Rule: The Only Difference Between Success and Failure by Grant Cardone

Good Boss, Bad Boss by Robert Sutton

Ogilvy on Advertising by David Ogilvy

The Likeability Factor by Tim Sanders

The Lean Startup by Eric Ries

Resonate by Nancy Duarte

A Mind of Its Own by Cordelia Fine

The Knowing-Doing Gap by Jeffrey Pfeffer, Robert I. Sutton

The SPEED of Trust by Stephen Covey

What Got You Here Won't Get You There by Marshall Goldsmith, Mark Reiter

Thinking, Fast and Slow by Daniel Kahneman

The Innovator's Dilemma by   Clayton Christensen

The Advantage: Why Organizational Health Trumps Everything Else in Business by Patrick Lencioni

Innovation is Everybody's Business by Robert B. Tucker

The 80/20 Principle: The Secret to Achieving More with Less by Richard Koch

Dealing with Darwin: How Great Companies Innovate at Every Phase of Their Evolution by Geoffrey Moore

Escape Velocity by Geoffrey Moore

Leading at a Higher Level by Ken Blanchard

A Sense of Urgency by John Kotter

Getting to Yes by Roger Fisher

Poke the Box by Seth Godin

Hard Facts, Dangerous Half-Truths and Total Nonsense by Jeffrey Pfeffer, Robert Sutton

Happy for No Reason by Marci Shimoff, Carol Kline

Tribal Leadership: Leveraging Natural Groups to Build a Thriving Organization by Dave Logan

Perfect Phrases for Dealing with Difficult Situations at Work by Susan Benjamin

The Power of Full Engagement by Jim Loehr, Tony Schwartz

Do More Great Work: Stop the Busywork by Michael Stanier

Business Writing: What Works, What Won't by Wilma Davidson

Essential Scrum by Kenneth Rubin

http://blogs.construx.com/blogs/stevemcc/archive/2008/03/27/productivity-variations-among-software-developers-and-teams-the-origin-of-quot-10x-quot.aspx

Acknowledgments

Special thanks to contributors, reviewers, and supporters Anand Padavala, Abhishikta Chava, Krista Todd, Teri Bommarito, Tony Lee, Joe Miller, Brandon Johnson, Mark Fiske, Ryan Park, Jim Yu, Brad Mattick, Mike Cammarata, Jamie Woo, and Riki Newton.

Very special thanks to Dave Lawson for the fortification and for coming up with the title.

Made in the USA
Monee, IL
23 March 2021